CONTENTS.

An F-35A of the 34th Fighter Squadron — a unit that has rarely been out of the headlines in 2017.
Jamie Hunter

EDITOR
Jamie Hunter
GROUP EDITOR
Nigel Price
DESIGN
Dominique Maynard
PRODUCTION MANAGER
Janet Watkins
ADVERTISING SALES
Ian Maxwell
ADVERTISING PRODUCTION
Debi McGowan
GROUP MARKETING MANAGER
Martin Steele
CIRCULATION & CONTRACT PUBLISHING EXECUTIVE
Amy Donkersley

COMMERCIAL DIRECTOR
Ann Saundry
PUBLISHER AND MANAGING DIRECTOR
Adrian Cox
EXECUTIVE CHAIRMAN
Richard Cox

PRINTED BY
Warners (Midlands) plc, The Maltings, Bourne, Lincs PE10 9PH (UK)

DISTRIBUTED BY
Seymour Distribution Ltd
2 Poultry Avenue,
London EC1A 9PP (UK)
+44(0)20 7429 4000

CONTACTS
Key Publishing Ltd
PO Box 100, Stamford,
Lincolnshire, PE9 1XQ, UK

Tel: +44 (0)1780 755131
Fax: +44 (0)1780 757261
E-mail :
enquiries@keypublishing.com
www.keypublishing.com

PUBLISHER
Key Publishing Ltd

Printed in England

A B-1B Lancer assigned to the 28th Bomb Wing, deployed from Ellsworth AFB, South Dakota, during a 10-hour mission from Andersen AFB, Guam, into Japanese airspace and over the Korean Peninsula. USAF/A1C Christopher Quail

WELCOME.

WELCOME TO THE third edition of the *US Air Force Air Power Yearbook*. This annual bookazine aims to deliver a roundup of the most exciting action from the ranks of the world's premier air arm.

Once again, readiness is at the forefront of the concerns for USAF leaders. It's a word that has many influencing factors, not least manpower — the USAF says it is short by nearly 2,000 pilots — hardware, funding, the list goes on. Ultimately, the biggest concerns as this magazine went to press were over sequestration; the threat of a funding freeze due to legal wrangling over formal budgets. It's something that Gen Dave Goldfein, the USAF chief, says would 'break' the service.

One of the ways the USAF is looking to retain and 'absorb' more pilots is through OA-X or light attack. This could see the USAF at long last buying a fleet of low-cost, light attack aircraft to operate in low-threat theaters in support of ground forces in the close air support role. It would also, importantly, serve to reduce the burden on over-worked fighter squadrons. The knock-on effect could be dramatic in helping reduce the strain on the squadrons, lowering flying rates on expensive high-end fighters, and increasing mass in a more cost-effective manner.

Ultimately, the USAF has been on constant combat operations for the past 26 years. In that time its size has fallen drastically. It's time to reverse that trend.

Jamie Hunter,
Editor
E-mail: jamie.hunter@keypublishing.com

UNITED STATES AIR FORCE AIR POWER YEARBOOK 2018

A B-52H Stratofortress high above Iraq during an Operation 'Inherent Resolve' mission. Despite being over 50 years old, the B-52s continue to provide sterling service to the USAF and will continue to do so for several decades to come. USAF/SSgt Michael Battles

STATE OF THE FORCE

In November, Secretary of the Air Force Heather Wilson and Chief of Staff Gen David Goldfein gave their State of the Air Force address, which touched on a number of important issues that are at the top of their list of concerns.

report: **Jamie Hunter**

I N 1991 WHEN Gen David Goldfein was a young Captain on the 17th Tactical Fighter Squadron going into combat in Operation 'Desert Storm', the US Air Force had 134 fighter squadrons. The war with Iraq saw 34 of those squadrons being forward deployed to the Middle East to tackle Saddam Hussein's military — a not insignificant opponent but not a 'near peer' adversary. Today, the USAF operates 55 squadrons total. Goldfein rightly says: 'There's no slack in the system. The force is stretched.'

Speaking alongside Secretary of the Air Force Heather Wilson at the Pentagon during the State of the Air Force address on November 9, the two most senior Air Force leaders were sounding a note of severe concern amid some very real problems that face their service.

Secretary Wilson said the USAF must have a higher and more stable budget to provide security for the nation. 'The fiscal 2018 Continuing Resolution is actually delaying our efforts to increase the readiness of the force, and risk accumulates over time. We are stretching the force to the limit, and we need to start turning the corner on readiness.

'If the Air Force goes through sequestration again, people will walk. Congress needs to lift sequestration as it is currently structured,' she said. Wilson also stressed the importance of cost-effective modernization of the force, driving innovation, developing leaders and strengthening America's alliances.

A force in crisis

'Surge has become the new normal,' Wilson said. 'Less than one per cent of Americans serve in uniform and protect the rest of us, and they're carrying a heavy burden. We are burning out our people because we are too small for what the nation is asking of us.'

Wilson referenced an Air Force member she had recently met who had just returned from their 17th deployment. 'They can't do it at this pace.'

The USAF has set up an Aircrew Crisis Task Force with eight lines of effort to try to address the problem of personnel retention. 'There is no one single thing we can do [to address this],' said Wilson. Last summer the USAF said it was 1,500 pilots short, and it expected the problem to only get worse. That prediction has come true — the latest

A relentless series of deployments as well as a raft of commitments at home keep the USAF's active-duty units extremely busy. USAF/SSgt Trevor T. McBride

Inset: Gen Goldfein addresses reporters on November 9. USAF

The pilot shortage is only getting worse for the USAF as it reflects a shortage across the board in the US. Jamie Hunter

B-1Bs operated by the 37th Expeditionary Bomb Squadron, escorted by F-15Js from the Japan Air Self-Defense Force carried out an over-water mission in international airspace east of North Korea on September 23. The mission was conducted further north of the Demilitarized Zone (DMZ) between North and South Korea than any US fighter or bomber aircraft have flown in recent history. USAF

fiscal year closed with the USAF being some 1,926 pilots short. With an overall tally of 20,000, it equates to a 10 per cent deficit. A lot of these are some of the Air Force's most experienced pilots.

Wilson quoted an F-22 pilot's father who told her that despite being the squadron Director of Operations, his son flies all the time because he's one of only three instructors on the unit. Gen Goldfein said the USAF needs to retain as many pilots as possible and build capacity, explaining that it takes a decade on average to train a fighter pilot. 'It takes $10 million per pilot to train them, so $10 billion of

capital investment walked out the door.' He added that he and the wider USAF is focused on this long-term, adding that in the US as a whole, across the military and commercial sectors, there simply aren't enough aviators to meet the demand. 'They stay [in the USAF] because they want to work with amazing people and they want to give their life meaning.' He said: 'If we're going to retain [people], it's about reconnecting the value proposition' — making personnel feel valued, respecting their service and the importance of what they do. Plus, of course, giving them a sensible work/life balance.

Goldfein said the USAF is also growing the pilot training pipeline from 1,200 annually to 1,400, and that he has also been authorized to welcome retirees back into the active-duty Air Force. He warned that personnel shortfalls could get so bad that squadrons need to be cut — no one wants to see that happen. Wilson further warned: 'If we go through

Above: **Secretary of the Air Force Heather Wilson and Gen Dave Goldfein.** USAF

Below: **Transport pilots are on the road continuously. Every three minutes an Air Mobility Command aircraft takes off or lands somewhere on the planet.** USAF/SSgt Michael Battles

'If we can't move past sequester in its present form we will break this force'

sequester again, a 2,000-pilot shortage will be a dream. People will walk!' She added that the USAF still hasn't fully recovered from the last period of sequestration.

The service is making the mission happen, but on the backs of its airmen, Goldfein added. 'We are looking for ways to reduce the tension on the force.' Wilson and Goldfein both recognized the commitment airmen and families are making in service to the nation and advocated for Congress to provide the resources needed to sustain global operations. 'It's beyond pilots and aircrews, it's also the maintainers,' Goldfein said. 'When I started flying as a young F-16 pilot, I used to meet the crew chief for the walk round. You'd then have a last-chance crew. Nowadays

pilots have to taxi slow because the same crew chief has to drive to the end of the runway to pull the pins and arm the weapons. Then that same guy has to fly in a C-17 to the destination [to meet the fighters]. We are watching this with laser focus. Pilots that don't fly, maintainers that don't maintain, controllers that don't control, they will not stay with this company.'

Tools of the trade
Every dollar the USAF spends is focused on readiness and making the service more lethal, Goldfein says. As the service with the most diverse portfolio, the Air Force is involved in every joint force mission. 'Each of these missions is a growth industry, and every mission is no fail. Though airmen make carrying out

these missions look easy, it's anything but,' Goldfein added, while noting that the high operations tempo is taking its toll. 'Every three minutes an air mobility aircraft takes off or lands somewhere on the planet. We just flew over 14,000 sorties in the last three months alone simultaneously supporting Secretary [of State] Tillerson in the pressure campaign against North Korea, global operations in Europe and the Middle East and hurricane relief in Texas, Florida and Puerto Rico.'

Heather Wilson says it's not just pilots that are in short supply, it's also spare parts, flying hours and munitions. She called for 'cost-effective modernization'. 'The B-21 is on track, we have 120 operational F-35As and our focus is to drive down the cost of production and sustainment.' She also said that there was a need to drive innovation and referenced a new 12-month review of science and technology strategy. Fielding rapid capabilities is something that Air Force leaders repeatedly refer to — going from the 'lab to flight line' much quicker. 'The Light Attack Experiment is one of the ways we are trying to do things differently,' she said, in response to a question about the

$400 million put aside for OA-X, the USAF's possible new close air support aircraft. This experiment to test the feasibility, the need and the potential for a new aircraft started with a one-page letter from Goldfein to industry in March and by the summer four aircraft were at Holloman for the trial. Whilst it was arguably something of a poor showing in response, and two of the types have been heavily studied before, Wilson said she expects the completed report by the end of the year — 'we expect to make decisions from there,' she said.

Adding some detail, Gen Goldfein commented: 'There's two parallel paths we're looking at on light attack. One is the traditional hardware; the aircraft, sensor and weapons. There's another part of that which is the network that it rides on. As we bring more and more exquisite technology to the battlefield it actually becomes harder and harder to share information with our allies and partners who don't have the same level of technology. So the question we are asking is not only is there a light attack capability off-the-shelf that we can use that can increase lethality and readiness, but also is there a shareable network that allies and partners that are already

This image: **The USAF is looking to farm out aggressor services to help improve its training.** Jim Haseltine

Below: **With its diverse range of missions, the USAF needs to grow in size to meet the demand. Members of the 816th Expeditionary Airlift Squadron are depicted here boarding a C-17 Globemaster III at Al Udeid Air Base, Qatar, for a mission in support of Operation 'Inherent Resolve'.** USAF/SSgt Michael Battles

Bottom left to right: **The wear and tear on this F-15E is obvious to see, despite the fact that this is a relatively new platform when compared to other fourth-generation USAF fighters.** USAF/SSgt Michael Battles

The Light Attack Experiment at Holloman AFB in the summer included the Textron AirLand Scorpion. Textron/Jim Haseltine

Right page: **The last time sequestration kicked in, many USAF squadrons were grounded. It's a scenario that could break the Air Force if it happened again.** USAF/ SSgt Daryn Murphy

with us and those that may choose to join us [can use] in the campaign against violent extremism? Can we get into a new shareable network that allows information to flow at a far faster rate so we can take out the enemy?' He added that the aim is to push this extremist violence down to a level where local governance and local forces can handle it without the need for US assistance. He offered the question: 'How can light attack contribute to that?'

There can be little doubt that the OA-X initiative has some export intent in mind. The Textron AirLand Scorpion, for example, has attained a degree of credibility by the USAF including it in the experiment. The USAF is a linchpin in providing equipment and support to US allies, which recently included the delivery of the first F-35s to Norway, Lebanon's stateside A-29 Super Tucano training and Bahrain's $2.7-billion F-16V deal. 'Those partnerships we are creating with our allies, [as well as our] training, equipment and information exchange make the United States stronger because we're stronger when we're together,' Wilson said.

Budget woes

Ultimately, it's the current budget instability that is causing Goldfein and Wilson the biggest headaches. 'If we can't move past sequester in its present form we will break this force,' warned Gen Goldfein. The indecision over the future years funding allocations has already taken its toll. USAF Under Secretary Matt Donovan has said that the contract for the T-X trainer competition to replace the T-38 Talon will not now be awarded until the spring. Plans originally called for the award to be made before the end of 2017, however the schedule is moving to the right, even if Congress passed the spending bill that is currently holding back new programs. 'Source selection is never based on the calendar,' said Donovan, adding that March 2018 is now looking likely for a T-X decision. Wilson had already warned that the USAF would be unable to move ahead on new projects if the Continuing Resolution was still in place — which prohibits awarding new program contracts unless Congress approves specific funding. However, she hit a note of optimism: 'we expect to start production in FY18,' she said of

Above: **The T-50A is Lockheed Martin's offering for the T-X competition, the winner of which will now be revealed in 2018.** Lockheed Martin

Below: **The USAF is looking to increase pilot production from 1,200 to 1,400 pilots annually.** USAF/SSgt Keith James

T-X. 'The RFP [Request For Proposals] is event based, not schedule based. We don't expect an impact on the production timeline.'

The Continuing Resolution Appropriations Bill was set to expire on December 8 and another was expected to follow. Without an agreement on the FY 2018 defense budget, sequestration and strict defense spending caps would return by law. This is the disaster scenario that Wilson and Goldfein fear. It would halt new projects and contracts as well as having a massive knock-on effect on the wider operations of this stretched force.

CAPABLE.
VERSATILE.

TEXTRON AVIATION
DEFENSE

AFFORDABLE.

SCORPION
SEE + SENSE + STING

SCORPIONJET.COM | U.S. **+1.844.44.TXTAV** | INTERNATIONAL **+1.316.517.8270**

UNITED STATES AIR FORCE

A YEAR IN REVIEW

Combat Aircraft reviews the major news stories from around the USAF in 2017.

SPIRITS STRIKE ISLAMIC STATE

GLOBAL POWER RAIDS ON TERROR CAMPS

TWO B-2AS OPERATED by the 509th Bomb Wing conducted precision air strikes on a pair of training camps of the so-called Islamic State (IS) near Sirte, Libya, during a 30-plus-hour mission on January 18, 2017. The strike reportedly killed as many as 80 to 100 enemy fighters. The Spirits, which flew the round trip to Libya from Whiteman Air Force Base, Missouri, struck the targets with precision-guided 500lb (227kg) GBU-38 Joint Direct Attack Munitions (JDAMs). The operation was supported by 15 KC-135 and KC-10 tankers from five bases.

In related news, three B-2As operated by crews from the 393rd Bomb Squadron and the Missouri Air National Guard's 110th Bomb Squadron also completed a three-week deployment to Andersen AFB, Guam in support of the US Strategic Command's (USSTRATCOM) Bomber Assurance and Deterrence mission. The bombers had been deployed to Guam along with around 200 personnel from the 509th and 131st Bomb Wings, on January 9. While operating from Andersen, the B-2As carried out local and long-duration sorties throughout the Indo-Asia-Pacific region that included training with regional partners including the Australian Air Operations Centre and Australian Joint Terminal Attack Controllers. The bombers also conducted an integrated exercise with US Navy forces and F-22As operated by the Hawaii Air National Guard's 154th Wing near Oahu.

A B-2 Spirit is readied at Whiteman AFB, Missouri, for the raid on Libya. USAF/SrA Joel Pfiester

T-X DELAYED

BUDGET CONCERNS AND MORE QUESTIONS PUSH PROGRAM INTO 2018

NEW US AIR Force Under-Secretary Matt Donovan has said that a decision on the T-X trainer competition to replace the T-38 Talon will likely not be made until the spring. Plans called for a winner to be named before the end of 2017, but this now looks unlikely. Even if Congress has passed a US defense spending bill that is currently holding back new programs, T-X looks set to be delayed. 'Source selection is never based on the calendar,' said Donovan, adding that March 2018 is now looking likely for a T-X decision.

The news comes as no great surprise, given that Air Force Secretary Heather Wilson had already warned that the USAF would be unable to move ahead on new projects if the continuing resolution was still in place. It prohibits awarding new program contracts unless Congress approves specific funding.

The USAF has also said it needs more time to evaluate information from the competing vendors. Boeing, Lockheed Martin, Leonardo DRS and maybe the SNC Corporation are in the running to supply 350 new trainers for the USAF.

Meanwhile, Boeing and its partner Saab say they will establish a manufacturing and production facility in the US for their clean-sheet T-X aircraft. The Swedish company says it has started the process to evaluate and identify potential locations for production. 'The Boeing and Saab T-X is designed and purpose built for the USAF training mission, so we believe that the entire aircraft, including our part, should also be manufactured in the US', said Håkan Buskhe, President and CEO of Saab AB. 'Saab has already invested in the development of the T-X advanced trainer aircraft and if Saab and Boeing win, Saab will carry that commitment a step forward into manufacturing and production in the US.'

Boeing has already stated that it will conduct final assembly of its T-X aircraft at its St Louis, Missouri, facility if it wins the USAF contract, and that this would support approximately 1,800 jobs in the region. The agreement with Saab and suppliers means that around 90 per cent of the Boeing offering will be manufactured in the US.

There is little doubt that bringing Saab on board has enhanced Boeing's ability to demonstrate rapid design, development and production skills through the cost-effective realization of its clean-sheet design. 'Our highly skilled St Louis workforce designed, assembled, and brought Boeing T-X to life and they continue to define the future, not just for our company, but for our customers and the global aerospace industry', said Shelley Lavender, St Louis senior executive and President of Boeing Military Aircraft. Saab has repeatedly demonstrated the use of cutting-edge technologies to deliver relevant technology, but also to minimize the impact of flight-testing through the use of new production techniques to help bring down cost and leverage efficiencies.

The Boeing T-X has been designed specifically for the USAF training requirement to replace the service's fleet of aging T-38 Talons. The initial acquisition, for 350 aircraft and the associated ground-based training and support, is valued at up to $16 billion. Initial operating capability is planned for 2024.

Leonardo announced in 2017 the selection of Moton Field in Tuskeegee, Alabama, as the site for a production facility where it would build T-100 trainer jets if the aircraft is selected by the US Air Force. The contractor would invest $200-250 million in infrastructure and equipment and would employ around 750 workers at the facility. Production of the trainer would be undertaken by Leonardo's DRS USA subsidiary. Leonardo had previously been partnered with Raytheon, which had chosen a site in Meridian, Mississippi for its production facility.

The two Boeing T-X prototypes (N381TX and N382TX) fly over St Louis, Missouri. Boeing

UPGRADED SENTRY DELIVERED

FIRST DRAGON E-3 FOR USAF ARRIVES AT TINKER AFB

THE FIRST E-3 Sentry aircraft to be upgraded with a 'glass' flight deck modification under the Diminishing Manufacturing Sources Replacement of Avionics for Global Operations and Navigation (DRAGON) arrived at Tinker Air Force Base, Oklahoma on January 9, 2017. The Sentry is the first of 24 modified E-3s that will receive the modifications over the next eight years. The upgrades ensure that the aircraft is compliant with current and future international and domestic air traffic control requirements and allow the aircraft to access Reduced Vertical Separation Minimum airspace and optimal flight levels, increasing fuel efficiency and reducing clearance delays.

It also replaces analog technology with commercially viable digital flight management systems. The new avionics include five color multi-function displays that can display engine, navigation and radar data. Additionally, DRAGON adds the Mode 5 Identification Friend or Foe and provides Automatic Dependent Surveillance — Broadcast capabilities that increase situational awareness and enhance flight safety. The new systems also eliminate the need for a navigator.

E-3G serial 77-0351 touches down at Tinker AFB, Oklahoma on January 9. The aircraft is the first of 24 Sentries to receive the DRAGON cockpit modifications. USAF/Kelly White

LIGHTNING HITS THE ROAD

US AIR FORCE F-35A DEPLOYS TO EUROPE

SIX F-35A LIGHTNING IIs operated by the 388th Fighter Wing's 34th Fighter Squadron 'Rams' and the Air Force Reserve 419th Fighter Wing's 466th Fighter Squadron at Hill AFB, Utah, arrived at RAF Lakenheath, UK, on April 15, 2017 at the start of the type's first overseas training deployment to Europe. The fighters conducted training operations with other Europe-based aircraft for several weeks in support of the European Reassurance Initiative. RAF Lakenheath was a likely deployment location since it will be the first overseas beddown location for the F-35A. As part of the deployment, the F-35As also forward deployed to NATO nations to 'maximize training opportunities, build partnerships with allied air forces, and become familiar with Europe's diverse operating conditions'.

Tankers from four different bases including the 100th Air Refueling Wing at RAF Mildenhall, UK, offloaded more than 400,000lb of fuel to the fighters in support of the deployment. The deployment was also supported by C-17 and C-5 airlifters that moved maintenance equipment and personnel.

'This is an incredible opportunity for USAFE airmen and our NATO allies to host this first overseas training deployment of the F-35A aircraft,' said Gen Tod Wolters, US Air Forces in Europe, Air Forces Africa commander. 'As we and our F-35 partners bring this aircraft into our inventories, it's important that we train together to integrate into a seamless team capable of defending the sovereignty of allied nations. Lakenheath will be the first overseas beddown location for the F-35A [and] this deployment allows our pilots and maintainers to learn more about the European operating environment and will improve interoperability with our partners.'

F-35A serial 13-5072 from the 34th Fighter Squadron touches down at RAF Lakenheath, UK, on April 15. The six aircraft comprised serials 13-5072, 14-5094, 14-5096, 14-5097, 14-5098, 14-5102. USAF/MSgt Eric Burks

NEW LOCATIONS FOR REAPERS, LIGHTNING IIs AND PEGASUS NAMED

The USAF has selected Shaw AFB, South Carolina, as the preferred location for basing a new MQ-9 group that will stand up in Fiscal 2018. The group will include mission control elements (MCE), however, Reapers will not be stationed at or flown from Shaw. The service has selected Davis-Monthan AFB, Arizona; Moody AFB, Georgia; Mountain Home AFB, Idaho; and Offutt AFB, Nebraska, as reasonable alternatives and the bases will be considered as part of the environmental impact analysis process. The Air Force is still considering locations that will host a complete Reaper wing that will includes as many as 24 MQ-9s, launch and recovery elements (LRE), an MCE, a maintenance group and support personnel.

Shaw remains under consideration for that mission along with Eglin AFB and Tyndall AFB in Florida and Vandenberg AFB, California. Selection of that location has still to be determined.

Naval Air Station Fort Worth Joint Reserve Base, Texas, has been selected by the USAF as the preferred location for the first Air Force Reserve Command-led F-35A unit. The command's 301st Fighter Wing, which currently operates the F-16C, is expected to receive its first Lightning IIs in the mid-2020s. The service will consider Davis-Monthan AFB, Arizona; Homestead Air Reserve Base, Florida; and Whiteman AFB, Missouri, as reasonable alternatives during the environmental analysis process,

which must be completed before a final basing decision can be made. It is currently evaluating five Air National Guard facilities as part of a plan to determine the next two units that will receive the F-35A.

The service will announce its preferred and reasonable alternatives for the ANG bases this summer and F-35As are expected to begin arriving at the second and third ANG locations in the early to mid-2020s.

USAF officials selected Joint Base McGuire-Dix-Lakehurst, New Jersey, and Travis AFB, California, as the preferred locations for the next two active-duty-led KC-46A tanker units. A total of 48 KC-46As will replace the fleet of KC-10As assigned to the 305th and 22nd

Air Mobility Wings at the two bases.

The USAF will consider Fairchild AFB, Washington, and Grand Forks AFB, North Dakota, as reasonable alternatives during the environmental impact analysis process. The first KC-46As are expected to arrive at the new locations in 2019. Once the fleet size is increased to 479 tankers, the USAF will begin phasing out its legacy tanker aircraft. Altus AFB, Oklahoma; McConnell AFB, Kansas; Pease Air National Guard Station, New Hampshire; and Seymour Johnson AFB, North Carolina; were previously named as future KC-46 basing locations. Delivery of the first of 33 KC-46As to McConnell and Altus has been delayed to spring 2018.

MOAB COMBAT DEBUT

An Air Force Special Operations Command MC-130 delivered a GBU-43 Massive Ordnance Air Blast (MOAB), also known as the 'Mother of All Bombs', during an air strike on a so-called Islamic State (IS) tunnel complex in the Achin district of Afghanistan's Nangarhar province, on April 13. The mission marked the combat debut for the United States' most powerful non-nuclear bomb. Developed in just nine weeks to support the Iraq war in 2003, the MOAB had not previously been used in combat. The 30ft (9.1m), GPS-guided bomb weighs 21,000lb (9,525kg) and carries 18,000lb (8,165kg) of explosives in its BLU-120/B warhead.

'The strike was designed to minimize the risk to Afghan and US forces conducting clearing operations in the area while

maximizing the destruction of ISIS-K [Khorasan] fighters and facilities,' US Forces-Afghanistan said in a statement. The Afghan Ministry of Defense said that 36 IS fighters were killed in the strike, with no civilian casualties reported.

The strike came as US and coalition aircraft had a record month in March, dropping 3,878 bombs on IS targets Iraq and Syria under Operation 'Inherent Resolve'. It marked the highest tally since the operation started in 2014. The increase in activity came as Iraqi Security Forces pushed further into IS-held western Mosul, and US-backed rebels in Syria attempt to close in on the IS capital city of Raqqa. In Afghanistan, US aircraft released 203 weapons, the highest since October 2016.

F-16 TESTS NEW NUCLEAR BOMB

An F-16C from the 422nd Test and Evaluation Squadron (TES) at Nellis AFB, Nevada, dropped an inert B61-12 nuclear bomb on the Nevada Test and Training Range (NTTR) in March. The test was used to evaluate the weapon's arming and fire control system, radar altimeter, spin rocket motors, and weapons control computer, according to

an April news release. The B61-12 is a new version of the B61 air-launched nuclear bomb. 'The B61-12 gravity bomb ensures the current capability for the air-delivered leg of the US strategic nuclear triad well into the future for both bombers and dual-capable aircraft supporting NATO,' commented Paul Waugh of the Air Force Nuclear Weapons Center.

An F-16C of the 422nd TES carrying the new B61-12 in recent testing. USAF

THUNDERBIRD UPGRADES

The Block 52 F-16Cs operated by the USAF Air Demonstration Squadron will be the first Air Force fighters to undergo the Service Life Extension Program (SLEP) and one of the team's 11 aircraft has already entered the program. The

SLEP is being carried out by the Ogden Air Logistics Complex at Hill AFB, Utah. The Thunderbird's aircraft were selected because they are subjected to greater stresses due to the nature of their demonstration mission.

USAF

BONEYARD BOUND

The USAF's oldest C-5A departed Westover Air Reserve Base on April 20, en route to Davis-Monthan AFB, Arizona, where it was placed in storage with the 309th Aerospace Maintenance and Regeneration Group (AMARG). Serial 69-0020 was one of four remaining Galaxy airlifters in service with the Air Force Reserve Command's 439th Airlift Wing that will not be upgraded to C-5M standard and had accumulated more than 21,000 flight hours since entering service in November 1971. Two of the wing's three remaining C-5As were sent to the Tucson base in summer 2017 and one was transferred to the Travis Heritage Center at Travis AFB, California. The last of the three C-5As at Westover was retired to AMARG on September 7.

The oldest C-5A in the USAF fleet departs Westover Air Reserve Base, Massachusetts, on April 20 for the boneyard at Davis-Monthan AFB in Tucson, Arizona. The departure of serial 69-0020 left the 439th Airlift Wing with just three C-5As on its ramp. Air Force Reserve Command

RAPTOR CONDUCTS MISSILE TESTS

F-22A Raptors operated by the US Air Force's 411th Flight Test Squadron at Edwards Air Force Base, California, completed developmental tests of the Raytheon AIM-9X Block II and AIM-120D air-to-air missiles on April 18. The Raptors launched inert missiles against multiple BQM-167A sub-scale aerial targets at the Utah Test and Training Range (UTTR). The tests were conducted as part of the F-22A's Block 3.2B upgrade developmental test and evaluation. The Block 3.2B modernization update to the F-22A is the largest capability upgrade for the Raptor since it reached initial operating capability in December 2005. In addition to Block 3.2B upgrades, the USAF is also developing datalink improvements for the Raptor along with software updates that will allow the F-22A and F-35A sensor packages to be connected.

Two F-22As operated by the 411th Flight Test Squadron conduct developmental tests associated with the Block 3.2B upgrade on May 5. Lockheed Martin/Chad Bellay

EPAWSS SUCCESS

The BAE Systems Eagle Passive/Active Warning Survivability System (EPAWSS) electronic warfare (EW) project completed a Critical Design Review in mid-2017, which was conducted by Boeing. The system is planned as a replacement for the Tactical Electronic Warfare System on more than 400 USAF F-15Cs and F-15Es. BAE Systems was selected by Boeing to develop the new EW system in October 2015. EPAWSS will initially be integrated on eight F-15s and flight-testing will begin in late 2018 under the new Suite 9 software release. The system is a key element of the upgrades Boeing has proposed to keep the F-15C viable until at least 2040. Boeing received a $478-million contract for the program's engineering manufacturing and development phase in October 2016.

In 2017 Boeing and the USAF also conducted a demonstration of the contractor's pod-mounted Talon HATE airborne networking system, which allows multiple aircraft and ground stations to efficiently and securely communicate in real-time. For the demonstration, which was carried out at Nellis AFB, Nevada, Talon HATE pods were installed on two F-15Cs. The pods enabled test pilots to share information through the military's Link 16, Common Data Link, and Wideband Global SATCOM satellite and validated intra-flight datalink network capabilities used by F-22s. The system allows pilots to transmit information quickly between the F-15C and other Air Force aircraft and weapon systems. Additional tests are currently demonstrating secure datalink connections between F-15Cs and F-22As.

FIRST AIR GUARD COMBAT KING II DELIVERED

The first HC-130J for the Alaska Air National Guard's 176th Wing arrived at Joint Base Elmendorf-Richardson on June 3 at the conclusion of a flight that began at Lockheed Martin's Greenville, South Carolina, facility on June 1. The Combat King II is the first of four that will be assigned to the wing's 211th Rescue Squadron. The squadron had previously operated the HC-130N version of the legacy Combat King. Its last example of that model was transferred to the Air Force Reserve Command's 920th Rescue Group at Patrick AFB, Florida, in January.

The Combat King II features improved navigation, threat detection and countermeasures systems as well as a fully integrated inertial navigation and global positioning system, and interior and exterior lighting compatible with night-vision goggles. Additionally, the aircraft feature electro-optical/infra-red sensors, radar and missile warning receivers, chaff and flare dispensers, satellite and data-burst communications, and the ability to receive fuel in flight via a Universal Aerial Refueling Receptacle Slipway Installation.

HC-130J serial 14-5815 is the first of four Combat King IIs to be delivered to the Alaska Air National Guard's 176th Wing at Joint Base Elmendorf-Richardson, Alaska. Lockheed Martin

C-5M TRAINING RELOCATES

The C-5M Formal Training Unit (FTU) conducted its final training flight at Dover AFB, Delaware, on June 8. Future Super Galaxy training will be conducted by the Air Force Reserve Command's (AFRC) 433rd Airlift Wing at Joint Base San Antonio-Lackland Kelly Field Annex in Texas. Although the FTU has been in place at Dover since 2012, it was never meant to operate permanently from the Delaware base.

The transition to Lackland, which had previously been responsible for legacy C-5A/B training, began in 2016. Training at Dover had been carried out by instructors from the 9th Airlift Squadron, which was augmented by the AFRC's co-located 709th Airlift Squadron.

NEW RADAR FOR VIPERS

The USAF has awarded Northrop Grumman a $244-million contract to provide 72 AN/APG-83 Scalable Agile Beam Radar (SABR) active electronically scanned array (AESA) radars that will replace the current AN/APG-68 mechanically scanned radar installed on Air National Guard F-16Cs that support the air defense mission. The service began looking for a new radar to equip the fighters in response to a US Northern Command (NORTHCOM) Joint Emergent Operational Need to counter new threats to the American homeland that have emerged in recent years. The APG-83 will enable smaller target detection, greater targeting range and the ability to engage multiple targets, greatly increasing the F-16's capabilities against sophisticated threats that include new enemy cruise missiles and advanced fighters.

Utilizing technology developed for the F-35's AN/APG-81, the SABR can detect, track and identify a greater number of targets more quickly and at longer ranges than the APG-68. The system also has much higher resolution than the current radar and is capable of operating in conditions where heavy jamming is encountered. Additionally, it features an all-weather, high-resolution synthetic aperture radar mapping capability that provides the pilot with an all-weather, high-resolution surface image for precision target identification and strikes. Delivery of the first radar systems is expected to begin in December 2018.

USAF CONSIDERS NEW TRAINING BASE

With plans to expand its annual training of new pilots, the USAF's Air Education and Training Command (AETC) is reportedly conducting a study to determine whether it needs to stand up another Undergraduate Pilot Training (UPT) wing and where it could be located. UPT is currently carried out at Columbus AFB, Mississippi; Vance AFB, Oklahoma; Laughlin AFB and Sheppard AFB in Texas. The service had conducted the UPT mission at Williams AFB, Arizona and Reese AFB, Texas, but both of those bases were closed following the recommendations of the 1991 and 1995 Base Realignments and Closures (BRAC) commissions in September 1993 and September 1997. As a result the mission will likely be assigned to an existing facility.

The command currently trains around 1,000 new pilots annually and will graduate 1,400 pilots each year beginning in October 2018. Due to an increasing shortage of pilots the USAF currently has a requirement for expanding pilot production, which is the driving force behind the study.

PREDATOR FLIES FINAL CENTCOM COMBAT MISSION

The 361st Expeditionary Attack Squadron flew its final MQ-1B mission within the US Central Command area of responsibility on July 1. The following day the squadron held a ceremony to mark the conclusion of operations of the remotely piloted aircraft (RPA). Since the unit was activated 18 months previously as the 361st Expeditionary Reconnaissance Squadron its Predators flew more than 2,000 combat missions, covering 36,000 flight hours, and fired 358 AGM-114 Hellfire missiles against so-called Islamic State targets. The USAF is phasing out the MQ-1B in favor of the more capable MQ-9A Reaper and plans to retire the Predators by 2018. In fact, the 432nd Wing at Creech AFB, Nevada, and the 49th Wing at Holloman AFB, New Mexico have already ended their Predator missions.

LAST EXTENDER UPGRADED

Rockwell Collins has completed the installation of new avionics on the USAF's fleet of 59 KC-10 Extender aerial refueling aircraft, the company announced in October. The installation of the Flight2 integrated avionics system was carried out under a six-year contract intended to make the Extenders compliant with new communications, navigation, surveillance and air traffic management systems (CNS/ATM) mandates for accessing global airspace.

The Flight2 suite integrates CNS equipment with new avionics, with sensors, radios, autopilot, aircraft systems and provides advanced displays. The new avionics provide the KC-10 flight crew with enhanced situational awareness and communications improvements and more direct flight routing, which contributes to reduced fuel consumption. The modifications were carried out by Field Aviation at its facility in Oklahoma City, Oklahoma.

FIRST HOLLOMAN QF-16 MISSION

The QF-16C full-scale aerial target (FSAT) took to the air at Holloman AFB, New Mexico, for its first mission on February 10. The manned sortie, flown by Lt Col Ronald King, marked a milestone for transition of Detachment 1, 82nd Aerial Targets Squadron from the QF-4 Phantom to the QF-16. The QF-16 achieved initial operating capability with the 82nd ATRS at Tyndall AFB, Florida, in September 2016 and the last QF-4 were retired in December. USAF/SrA Emily Kenney

'EINSTEIN BOX' REVEALED

Coverage of Exercise 'Northern Edge' in Alaska in May revealed a Lockheed Martin U-2 (80-1070) flight-testing a new open systems architecture system to boost battlespace awareness and reduce the data-to-decision timeline for the warfighter. It has now been revealed that this was part of a Skunk Works project to demonstrate open mission systems (OMS). A series of six flights performed at 'Northern Edge' concluded one of these research and development efforts called 'Project Hunter', which matured open systems

architecture technologies and demonstrated the ability to share data across dissimilar platforms in denied environments. 'This demonstration focused on advanced communications and interoperability between systems,' said Renee Pasman, director of mission systems roadmaps at Lockheed Martin's Skunk Works. 'We used a highly capable, high-altitude U-2 as a vital communications and processing node, connecting a web of systems across multiple domains and enabling complete battlespace awareness.'

At the heart of the system was an OSA mission computer, known as the 'Einstein Box'. 'Project Hunter' builds on the mission system integration work Lockheed Martin first demonstrated in 2013 and continues to advance with the U-2 OMS, as well as with 'Have Raider' (manned/unmanned teaming) and 'Project Missouri' (fourth- and fifth-generation fighter networking).

Earlier in 2017 the USAF said it would retain the Lockheed U-2S Dragon Lady past the previous 2019 end of service date. Reports in March suggested that the U-2 will be upgraded and retained until 2025 at least. Outgoing ACC commander Gen 'Hawk' Carlisle

said the USAF is trying to find the money to retain and upgrade the communications and sensors of the popular U-2.

Upgrades already in train include a Celestial Object Sighting System (COSS) plus a new Raytheon active electronically scanned array (AESA) upgrade for the advanced synthetic aperture radar system (ASARS), known as ASARS-2B. The U-2's electro-optical SYERS-2C imaging system has already been upgraded by UTC Aerospace Systems and the legacy Raytheon Remote Airborne Sensor RAS-1R SIGINT system has been replaced with the Northrop Grumman Airborne Signals Intelligence Payload (ASIP).

A U-2S with the OMS systems gets airborne from Joint Base Elmendorf-Richardson during 'Northern Edge'. USAF

USAF PURCHASES NEW AIR FORCE ONE AIRFRAMES

The USAF awarded Boeing a contract modification associated with the purchase of two commercial 747-8 aircraft that will be modified for use as new Presidential support aircraft. The aircraft will replace two VC-25As that are currently used for that role. The contract involves the delivery of two 747-8 series aircraft that had been ordered by Russian firm Transaero Airlines in December 2013 but were never delivered to the company, which filed for bankruptcy and ceased operations in October 2015.

The two 747-85Ms, which are currently assigned the Boeing test registrations N894BA (c/n

42416/1519) and N895BA (c/n 42417/1523), have been stored at the Southern California Logistics Airport in Victorville California, since February.

Boeing has been conducting risk reduction activities in support of the Presidential Airlift Recapitalization (PAR) program since July 2016. The USAF has already requested proposals from Boeing related to the design, modification, testing and fielding of the two Presidential support aircraft. Aircraft modifications are expected to begin in 2019 with the new aircraft reaching initial operational capability in 2024.

USAF CONSIDERS CHANGES TO ROTARY-WING TRAINING

As part of its effort to increase the production of fighter pilots and reduce a shortage of aviators, the USAF is considering eliminating training in the T-6A Texan II for prospective helicopter pilots. The service currently has a shortage of around 1,000 fighter pilots and according to Air Education Training Command (AETC) ending fixed-wing training for helicopter pilots would allow the T-6As to be used to train around 70-120 additional fighter pilots each year.

Although the T-6A training

helps the rotary-wing students better understand the flying environment, it is not essential to their success as a helicopter pilot. The elimination of T-6A training is one of several options being considered by the USAF's Aircrew Crisis Task Force. The rotary-wing students will still receive fixed-wing training as part of the Initial Flight Screening (IFS) program at Pueblo Memorial Airport, Colorado before moving to Fort Rucker, Alabama, where rotary-wing training is carried out by the 23rd Flying Training Squadron with the TH-1H.

NEW CAPABILITY FOR USAF EAGLES

Although uncertainly over the Fiscal 2018 Defense funding could delay the start of the project, Boeing and the USAF selected Lockheed Martin's Legion Pod infrared search and track (IRST) system for the F-15C. Plans call for the acquisition of 130 systems for integration with the Eagle fleet with initial operational capability planned for 2020. Boeing, which serves as the USAF's prime contractor for the F-15, will initially award Lockheed Martin an engineering, manufacturing, development and production contract and the first pods will be delivered in 2018. More than 25 test flights were carried out by F-15Cs and F-16Cs equipped with the pod to demonstrate its integration, detection and tracking capabilities. Based on the IRST21, the pod features the same sensor that is being integrated with the F/A-18E/F.

GHOSTRIDER REACHES OPERATIONAL CAPABILITY

Air Force Special Operations Command's AC-130J Ghostrider gunship marked a major developmental milestone when it achieved initial operating capability on September 30. The 1st Special Operations Group has received six Ghostriders and a schoolhouse has been activated but it is unlikely the new gunship will be deployed in combat in the near future. Citing operational commitments and the need to sufficiently train personnel to operate and maintain the aircraft, the AC-130J will not deploy for at least two years. The service has converted or begun conversion of 10 MC-130Js to AC-130J configuration. The first Block 20 AC-130J was delivered in July 2016. The Ghostrider is scheduled to achieve full operational capability in 2023 when the last of 37 examples has entered service.

COMBAT RESCUE HELICOPTER IN PRODUCTION

Sikorsky Aircraft has begun major assembly of the first HH-60W Combat Rescue Helicopter for the USAF at its production facility in Bridgeport, Connecticut. The aircraft is the first of four engineering and manufacturing development (EMD) models that will support testing. The program is currently three months ahead of schedule and the contractor hopes to a achieve the 'required assets available' in March 2020, which is around six months earlier than required by its contract.

The milestone requires the delivery of eight production helicopters comprising four operational mission and four training aircraft 69 months after contract award. Sikorsky expects the HH-60W to make its first flight by 2019 and the target date for initial operational capability is 2021. Based on the US Army's UH-60M airframe the HH-60W will feature several additions including a 660 gal (2,498l) internal auxiliary fuel tank, an aerial refueling capability and MX-10 EO/IR sensor.

B-21 DESIGN REVIEW COMPLETED

The B-21A Raider bomber program is making progress and the USAF and Northrop Grumman announced completion of a Preliminary Design Review in March. The milestone occurred just 19 months after the contract for the new bomber was awarded. According to the Director of the Air Force Rapid Capabilities Office the program is meeting its goals. The B-21A design team is integrating mature technologies on the bomber and 'leveraging lessons learned' from the B-2, F-22, and F-35. The design incorporates an open architecture that allows for easy introduction of future upgrades.

A B-1B from the 412th Test Wing at Edwards AFB, California, conducts the first delivery of a production representative, tactical configuration AGM-158C Long Range Anti-Ship Missile (LRASM) on August 17. USAF

LRASM SUCCESS

The USAF, US Navy and Lockheed Martin carried out the first successful delivery of a production representative, tactical configuration AGM-158C Long Range Anti-Ship Missile (LRASM) from a B-1B on August 17. The test, which was conducted over the Sea Range at Point Mugu, California, was carried out with a B-1B from the 412th Test Wing at Edwards AFB, California. After navigating through all planned waypoints, the missile transitioned to mid-course guidance and flew toward the moving maritime target using inputs from the onboard multimodal sensor. After descending to low altitude for final approach to target area, the LRASM positively identified and impacted the moving maritime target. Designed to detect and destroy specific targets within groups of ships using advanced technologies, the LRASM is a precision-guided, anti-ship stand-off missile based on the AGM-154 Joint Air-to-Surface Standoff Missile — Extended Range (JASSM-ER). Early operational capability for the LRASM with the B-1B will occur in 2018 and on follow on the F/A-18E/F in 2019.

E-8C UPGRADES PLANNED

Although the USAF officially continues to move forward with plans to recapitalize its existing fleet of 16 E-8C Joint Surveillance Target Attack Radar System (Joint STARS) aircraft, the service is working with Northrop Grumman to develop a roadmap for keeping the battle management command and control (BMC2) intelligence surveillance and reconnaissance (ISR) system relevant and flying through 2030. Part of that roadmap will include increasing the Joint STARS' radar ability to detect smaller targets and emerging threats. Additionally the USAF is looking to replace or upgrade the aircraft's existing central computers and avionics system to support global air traffic management (GATM) requirements. Because it had planned to replace the E-8C upgrades for the aircraft have not been a priority until now.

It is actually unclear what the future holds for the Joint STARS recap program, which now appears to be in limbo. The service, which had planned to replace the E-8C with a smaller platform based on a corporate jet airframe, now wants to explore alternate intelligence and surveillance platforms. The move apparently follows the results of a recent fuselage fatigue study that indicated that some E-8Cs could fly through 2034.

Officially the service is still moving forward with source-selection efforts for the recap; however, it continues 'to evaluate alternative approaches for battlefield command and control that could be more effective in high-threat environments.'

Under current plans the service will continue flying the E-8C through fiscal year 2023. Concerned over a BMC2 and ISR capability gap, elected officials have already introduced an amendment to the Senate version of the Fiscal 2018 defense authorization bill that would prohibit the service from cancelling the Joint STARS recap program unless the defense secretary unless certain requirements are met and prevent the retirement of any E-8Cs. The Air Force currently plans to carry out an Advanced Battle Management System Analysis of Alternatives (AOA) in 2018. The USAF was expected to award a contract for the JSTARS recap in 2018 with the new platform reaching initial operational capability by 2024.

Northrop Grumman, which is partnered with L3 Technologies, Boeing, and Lockheed Martin are currently competing for the $6.9-billion Joint STARS recapitalization program and plans call for the new aircraft to be operational in 2024. The Northrop Grumman and Lockheed Martin design are respectively based on the Gulfstream G550 and Bombardier Global 6000 business jets while Boeing is offering a modified version of its 737-700 airliner and teams have been working to mature their proposals under risk-reduction contracts for several years.

USAF PREPARES FOR LIGHT ATTACK COMBAT EVALUATION

Following a successful evaluation of potential light attack aircraft the USAF is reportedly making plans to move forward with a combat demonstration in the US Central Command's area of responsibility in 2018. The service will reportedly conduct the evaluations of the SNC/Embraer A-29A Super Tucano and the Beechcraft AT-6 Wolverine aircraft under its Combat Dragon III project.

The project follows the Air Force's light attack demonstration that was carried out at Holloman AFB, New Mexico, over the summer. A formal decision on whether to proceed with the mid-east deployment will be made by the end of 2017 once the service has secured around $100 million in funding required for the project. The deployment will help the service decide whether the acquisition of around 300 light attack aircraft makes sense. As part of the combat demonstration the USAF would evaluate the effectiveness of the aircraft's precision weapons, unguided munitions and guns as well as its maintainability and reliability.

COMPASS CALL UPDATE

The US Government Accountability Office (GAO) has denied protests by Boeing and Bombardier against its program to recapitalize the EC-130H Compass Call electronic warfare aircraft. The USAF had planned to allow L3 Technologies to select the airframe that will serve as the new Compass Call platform. Under its EC-X Compass Call recapitalization program the service plans to cross deck the communications-jamming equipment into new Gulfstream G550 airframes.

The service is planning to replace its fleet of 14 EC-130Hs with 10 G550s that will receive the equipment as part of a 're-host' program. The service has operated the EC-130H, which are managed by the Air Force's Big Safari group at Wright-Patterson AFB, Ohio, in this role since 1983. L3 has served as the prime contractor for Compass Call for the past 15 years.

Boeing and Bombardier both file protests against the program claiming that the 'apparent sole-source award' violated the 2017 National Defense Authorization Act's outline for the Compass Call recapitalization.

On September 7, just days after the GAO decision, the USAF confirmed that it awarded L3 Technologies a contract to begin integration of the equipment onto a G550 aircraft using the Airborne Early Warning airframe configuration.

Gulfstream 550s are already on the US military inventory and are operated in the VIP transport role by the US Army, Navy and USAF under the designation C-37B.

L3 Technologies recently selected the Gulfstream G550 Airborne Early Warning platform to host the USAF's Compass Call equipment that will be 'cross-decked' from the services EC-130H electric combat aircraft. Gulfstream Aersopace

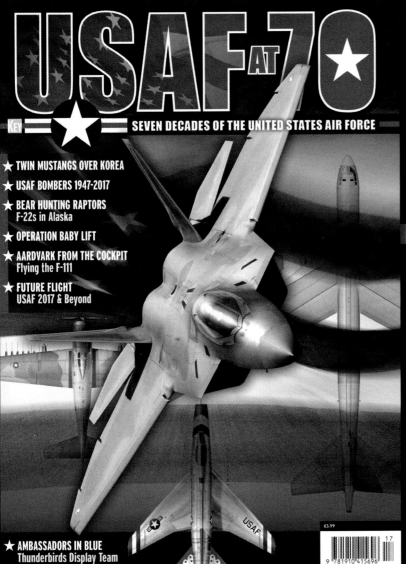

EXPERIMENT OR LIP SERVICE?

Initially dubbed OA-X, the USAF's Light Attack Experiment is designed to evaluate once and for all whether a new close air support platform might help reduce the burden on front-line fighter squadrons.

report: **Jamie Hunter with Jon Lake**

MANY SENIOR US Air Force officers see it as a throwback, an unnecessary waste of money, a retrograde step. In an era of tight budgets and advanced fifth-generation fighters for the near-peer fight why does the US Air Force need a new light attack aircraft? It's a quandary that the USAF has been embroiled in for over 50 years. However,

faced with huge pilot shortfalls, aging fighter fleets and spiraling operating costs, not looking at a new alternative to regularly deploying squadrons of F-15s and F-16s to meet close air support (CAS) needs would be, frankly, remiss.

The fact is that the USAF is regularly calling upon the likes of F-22 Raptors to make precision strikes in a low-threat theater of operations. While high-end fast jets offer a more versatile, multi-role club in the golf bag, it's tiring out squadrons

Above: **Embraer/ SNC A-29B Super Tucano demonstrator PT-ZNV flies during the Light Attack Experiment in August.** USAF/ Ethan D. Wagner

Inset right: **A member of the USAF evaluation team talks with a Textron Scorpion pilot at Holloman AFB on August 4.** USAF/ Christopher Okula

and forcing out experience to the stability of the airlines.

Despite the advice not to focus on the current war, the fact is that this type of operation has been going on for the last quarter of a century in the Central Command (CENTCOM) region — it's eaten up precious service life across the USAF fighter fleet. An on-call light attack turboprop aircraft with the requisite sensors and precision munitions can do most of the job an F-series fighter can in the CAS role. Ultimately, it's about getting an effect onto a target to meet the needs of the ground commander.

An A-29 Super Tucano may not have the dash speed of an F-16, but it sips fuel, and can stay on station without the need for tanker support, which is also in woefully short supply.

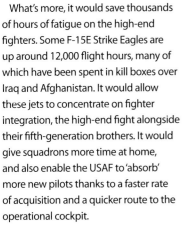

What's more, it would save thousands of hours of fatigue on the high-end fighters. Some F-15E Strike Eagles are up around 12,000 flight hours, many of which have been spent in kill boxes over Iraq and Afghanistan. It would allow these jets to concentrate on fighter integration, the high-end fight alongside their fifth-generation brothers. It would give squadrons more time at home, and also enable the USAF to 'absorb' more new pilots thanks to a faster rate of acquisition and a quicker route to the operational cockpit.

When it comes to combat operations, service life cannot be wasted on enduring, low-threat missions in a CAS 'wagon wheel'. Is it time for the USAF to look at a two-tiered approach? Does the defense budget allow it? As the US military faces a

The AT-6 has met the A-29 in competition in the past — the results of the Light Attack Evaluation will be critical to its future.
Beechcraft

renewed commitment in Afghanistan, the potential impact on US fighter squadrons is huge. Some say it should keep the fifth-gen' squadrons for the near-peer threat — and press a cheaper, lower tier, support platform into action when the risks remain low.

Combat Dragon

There has been a succession of recent attempts to field a low-cost light attack aircraft for the USAF, but none have succeeded. When the USAF evaluated the A-37 Dragonfly in Vietnam in 1967, the field test was nicknamed Combat Dragon. It was a moniker that was revived in 2015 as Combat Dragon II for a planned theater evaluation of the Embraer A-29 Super Tucano, but this ultimately saw a pair of OV-10 Broncos dispatched to CENTCOM for evaluation. In 2017 it was back again as

the service looked to send a pair of Super Tucanos and Beechcraft AT-6 Wolverines to South-west Asia under Combat Dragon III.

Back in 2008, Air Combat Command (ACC) launched OA-X to look at a potential solution that could be derived from a new platform to meet needs in irregular warfare. It called for an off-the-shelf design to ensure a more rapid development/evaluation/fielding cycle, and to reduce cost. It would be able to operate from austere forward operating bases and would need to be largely self-sustaining, since it would operate from bases where maintenance support would be lacking.

The OA-X Enabling Concept highlighted the need for advanced communications, including an option for a datalink, and an electro-optical/infra red sensor that would provide video via a ROVER-compatible datalink to enable emerging digital CAS

This image: OA-X is aimed at lightening the load on communities such as the F-15E Strike Eagle. Here, crews prepare Strike Eagles assigned to the 336th Expeditionary Fighter Squadron for sorties in support of Operation 'Inherent Resolve' In November.
USAF/SrA Joshua Kleinholz

capabilities. The aircraft would also be required to have a precision munitions capability.

It led to the issue of a Light Attack/Armed Reconnaissance (LAAR) Capability Request for Information (CRFI) on July 27, 2009. This initially envisaged a $2-billion purchase of 100 LAAR aircraft but was soon expanded to cover the acquisition of four squadrons (176 primary aircraft, 204 including backup aircraft inventory and attrition reserve) for $4.2 billion, with initial deliveries in Fiscal Year 2012.

Candidate aircraft included the Embraer Super Tucano, the Beechcraft AT-6B, the Air Tractor AT-802U, the Leonardo M-346 Master, Boeing's OV-10X Bronco and even the Pilatus PC-6 Turbo Porter.

The LAAR program was progressively scaled back in the face of budget cuts, and also as a result of growing political opposition to the probable selection of the Super Tucano — widely regarded as the strongest and most suitable candidate. The emphasis steadily shifted from American use of the aircraft toward building the capabilities of partner air forces.

As LAAR faltered, a parallel Light Air Support (LAS) program was established, aiming to procure a small number of light attack aircraft for use not by the USAF, but by the ANAAC (Afghan National Army Air Corps), with CENTCOM acting as the contracting authority.

In January 2011, a systems demonstration phase was held for both the A-29 and the AT-6B out of Kirtland AFB, New Mexico. It included austere evaluations at an airstrip in Truth or Consequences, New Mexico. In

Textron AirLand now has four Scorpions flying. This example, N532TX, has recently been at King Faisal Air Base, Tabuk, as Saudi Arabia evaluated the aircraft for close air support.
Textron AirLand/ Erik Hildebrandt

OV-10G+ BuNo 155492 that participated in the highly successful Combat Dragon II evaluation. Despite its popularity, Boeing has shied away from re-launching Bronco production.
Michael Keaveney

December 2011, Sierra Nevada received a $355.1-million firm-fixed price delivery order for 20 A-29 Super Tucano LAS aircraft and associated mission planning, training and support equipment. The aircraft were to be assembled by the Sierra Nevada Corporation in the US, and deliveries were to be completed by the end of April 2014.

The contract was cancelled after objections by Hawker Beechcraft, but Sierra Nevada won a subsequent competition, and was awarded a $427.5-million contract covering the delivery of 20 A-29s, plus associated mission planning, training and support equipment. The first aircraft was rolled out and handed over on September 25, 2014.

While the end of LAAR halted any immediate prospect of the US buying a light attack aircraft, there were a number of important US projects still running.

From 2008, the US Navy's 'Imminent Fury' program saw the evaluation of a single A-29 for supporting special operations teams in the field. The USAF was to have participated in a second phase, which was to have seen four A-29s deploying to Afghanistan from 2010, but the project reverted to the US Navy, and was redesignated as Combat Dragon II. This saw a lengthy evaluation of two OV-10G+ Broncos, initially in the US, but later including a combat deployment to the Middle East in 2015. The Broncos reportedly saw significant success against so-called Islamic State (IS) during Operation 'Inherent Resolve'.

From 2010, the US Air National Guard Air Force Reserve Command Test Center also began evaluating the first AT-6B in a congressionally funded technology demonstration of integrated ISR (intelligence, surveillance and reconnaissance) and weapons system capabilities. Several Air National Guard and Reserve Command A-10 and F-16 pilots gained significant experience of the AT-6.

All of this fed directly into a new light attack evaluation, which has covered a lot of the ground already well trodden in the LAS studies of 2011. Moreover, the intervening years have afforded an experienced cadre of combat-experienced USAF A-29 instructor pilots attached to the 81st Fighter Squadron at Moody AFB, Georgia, who have helped to train the Afghan (and now Lebanese) A-29 pilots.

Light attack re-born

In mid-2016, Lt Gen Mike Holmes, now the chief of ACC but then the USAF deputy chief of staff for strategic plans and requirements, reportedly said that his service was considering buying two CAS aircraft — 250 propeller-driven OA-X aircraft for use in 'permissive' environments, and an unknown number of A-X2 aircraft for use in more contested environments. He said the latter would not operate in the anti-access/area-denial (A2/AD) domain — that would remain the chosen arena for the F-35 and other more advanced platforms. While A-X2 sounded like an A-10 replacement for around 2025, OA-X clearly put the ball back in play for the A-29 and the AT-6.

'Working with industry, and building on the Combat Dragon series of tests, we are determining whether

a commercial off-the-shelf aircraft and sensor package can contribute to the coalition fight against violent extremism,' said USAF Chief of Staff Gen David Goldfein in 2017. Goldfein opened the door to aerospace contractors to join a new Light Attack Experiment, saying: 'this is not something we're looking to do a lot of research and development on. This is commercial, off-the-shelf technology that we can rapidly employ.'

The aircraft entered into the evaluation had to be able to perform light attack and armed reconnaissance missions by day and night, hitting stationary or moving targets using 500lb Paveway II weapons, aerial gunnery, and guided/unguided rockets, and with suitable secure tactical communications equipment. Survivability was to be assessed, including each platform's infra-red and visual signature, as well as weapons, sensor, and communications capabilities, and basic aerodynamic and austere field performance.

The requirement mandated that the aircraft should be able to operate from austere locations with unimproved surfaces, but at the same time, the take-off requirement was merely being able to clear a 50ft obstruction using a maximum runway length of 6,000ft — a far from stringent or challenging criteria! Converted crop-sprayers like the IOMAX Archangel and the Air Tractor/L3 OA-8 Longsword seemed to be well suited, but these options initially appeared to

> 'An A-29 Super Tucano may not have the dash speed of an F-16, but it sips fuel, and can stay on station without the need for tanker support, which is also in woefully short supply'

The Air Tractor/L3 OA-8 Longsword entered the experiment and was gauged as a 'Tier 2' aircraft as it did not meet all of the USAF's criteria.
L3 Communications

Above: **Textron AirLand claims that the Scorpion will cost less than $20 million, and, thanks to its extensive use of mature systems, will offer direct operating costs of less than $3,000 per hour.** USAF/Christopher Okula

Left top to bottom: **The A-29 drops a 500lb (227kg) laser-guided bomb during a demonstration flight over the White Sands Missile Range while participating in the Light Attack Experiment on August 1.** USAF/Ethan D. Wagner

The AT-6 Wolverine seen during the evaluation at Holloman in August. The previous light attack evaluation in 2011 saw both the AT-6 and A-29 operating from rough strips. USAF/Ethan D. Wagner

USAF test pilot Lt Col Lane Odom prepares to fly the A-29 during the Light Attack Experiment. USAF/Christopher Okula

have been removed from contention by the stated the need for tandem zero-zero ejection seats and for a pressurized cockpit (up to 25,000ft). Those setting out the requirements for the evaluation did lay down that any jet-engined contenders should have a 2.5-hr mission endurance (with appropriate fuel reserves, but using external fuel tanks if necessary — marking half the endurance required in the old OA-X Enabling Concept) and an average fuel flow of about 1,500lb/hr or less.

In the end, just four platforms entered the fray for the Light Attack Experiment, which began at Holloman AFB, New Mexico, on July 31. The experiment put each of the platforms through a series of exercises designed to test their capabilities in designated role.

Present at Holloman were the Embraer/Sierra Nevada A-29 Super Tucano, Beechcraft AT-6 Wolverine, L-3 Platform Integration Division/Air Tractor AT-802L Longsword and the twin-engine Textron AirLand Scorpion. For the purpose of the experiment, the A-29 and AT-6 were categorized as 'Tier One' because they met all of the objectives initially specified by the USAF. The Longsword and Scorpion were considered to be 'Tier 2' aircraft because they did not meet all of the objectives. According to Lt Gen Bunch, the Scorpion and Longsword were included because 'it's an experiment and we're trying something new, we wanted to open it up to industry.' The Longsword was allowed to participate despite being unpressurized and not equipped with ejection seats.

The USAF had set aside several of the requirements because of the small number of aircraft participating in the demonstration and the Longsword was in fact a last-minute addition to the experiment. Developed from Air Tractor's AT-802U crop-duster, the light attack and intelligence, surveillance and reconnaissance capable AT-802L features a digital 'glass' cockpit and is equipped with the L-3 Wescam MX-15 electro-optical/infra-red sensor and hardpoints under the wings and fuselage.

Run by the Air Force Strategic Development Planning and Experimentation Office at Wright-Patterson AFB, Ohio, the experiment was intended to rate the participant's ability to perform six missions that comprised basic surface attack (BSA), close air support (CAS), daytime ground assault force, rescue escort and night-time BSA and CAS.

Textron AirLand completed the first weapons firing trials with its company-funded Scorpion demonstrator — coincidentally also at Holloman — from October 10-14, 2016 with unguided Hydra 70 2.75in rockets, followed by four APKWS, and culminating with two live AGM-114F Hellfire missiles. Textron AirLand

Each of the aircraft were evaluated during multiple day and night missions.

USAF personnel directly associated with the evaluation included 16 aircrew, crew chiefs, maintainers, weapons personnel as well as Joint Terminal Attack Controllers (JTACs). The evaluating pilots had experience in the A-10C, F-16C, F-15E, F-22A, F-35A, U-28A, and B-52H. More than 580 data points included pilot workload to find and track a target, range scores, assessments of displays, capability in austere environments, cockpit visibility, loiter capability, communications, target tracking, lines of sight, sensor tracking, take-off distance, acoustic signatures

and weapons delivery. Inert weapons were delivered on the US Army White Sands Missile Range and other sites around Holloman. Some of the aircraft also operated from an undeveloped, dirt runway at Cannon AFB, New Mexico, as part of the austere environment evaluation.

Following completion of the Holloman evaluation the USAF said it was making plans to move forward with a combat demonstration in CENTCOM in 2018. The service will reportedly fly the Super Tucano and the Wolverine under the Combat Dragon III project. Two of each type will reportedly deploy with

Below: Lt Col Terrance Keithley, right, a test pilot for the 416th Flight Test Squadron at Edwards AFB, receives pre-flight briefing information from an instructor pilot for the AT-6 during the Light Attack Experiment. USAF/Ethan D. Wagner

70 people, according to Col Michael Pietrucha, the light attack advisor to ACC. Interestingly, Col Pietrucha was also the staff lead who helped draft the original OA-X requirements in 2008.

A formal decision on whether to proceed with the Middle East deployment was expected to be made by the end of 2017 once the service had secured around $100 million in funding required to move forward. The deployment should ultimately finalize whether the USAF will acquire 300 new light attack aircraft, or whether this has just been another round of drumming up international interest for new exports to nations in the region.

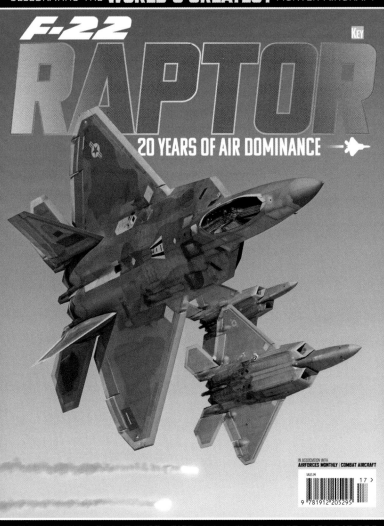

UNIT REPORT

A mountain flying course, a specialist firefighting role, disaster relief missions, not to mention its regular airlift mission — the 192nd Airlift Squadron 'High Rollers' of the Nevada Air National Guard is a unit with a diverse and impressive mission.

report: **Jamie Hunter**

'Roller 31', a C-130H3 of the Nevada ANG's 192nd AS, flies near Mount Whitney, California. All photos Jamie Hunter unless credited otherwise

HAVING RETIRED THE US Air Force's last RF-4C recce Phantoms in 1995, the 192nd Airlift Squadron 'High Rollers' has been in the C-130 Hercules business for over 20 years. Today it flies eight C-130H3s under the 152nd Airlift Wing out of Reno-Tahoe International Airport, Nevada, and fulfils an incredibly diverse range of missions.

The standard day-to-day Hercules roles are all on the flying schedule at the 'High Rollers' — from airlift to disaster relief. Indeed, when the *Yearbook* spoke to the unit's Lt Col Ricardo 'Finch' Bravo in October the squadron had two aircraft detached to the Caribbean on hurricane relief missions and had recently returned from similar efforts in Texas following Hurricane 'Harvey'.

What makes the 'High Rollers' particularly stand out are two highly specialized roles, which have been acquired thanks to the enthusiasm and experience of the resident personnel.

In 2016, after several years of lobbying, the 192nd took on the airborne firefighting role with the roll-on/roll-off Modular Airborne Fire Fighting System (MAFFS II). In addition, a homegrown mountain flying course has drawn the attention of the entire USAF Hercules community. The resulting Advanced Mountain Airlift Tactics School (AMATS) is now one of the most important C-130 flying courses in the world. Lt Col Bravo is the AMATS Director. 'We run four classes per year, one in January, a March class, one in June and another in October.' The October course brought one C-130H2 with a crew from the 357th AS at Maxwell-Gunter AFB, Alabama, and two C-130Js from the 815th AS at Keesler

AFB, Mississippi. 'Demand for the course is through the roof,' says Lt Col Bravo. 'In the future, we hope to run more than four courses per year'.

Advanced Mountain Airlift Tactics School (AMATS)

Primary AMATS instructor and co-ordinator is Maj Joseph 'Spock' Jaquish. 'The idea of a mountain flying course came up because a lot of C-130 squadrons were coming to Reno to inter-fly with us in our local terrain to prepare for their forthcoming deployments. They asked us for a local area briefing about flying in the mountains. After that happened a few times we talked about starting a formal

HIGH ROLLERS

mountain flying course because a lot of those units came here and found themselves in hazardous situations they weren't prepared for.'

Since August 1996 there have been eight C-130 controlled flight into terrain (CFIT) mishaps in hazardous environments. Within the same timeframe, US C-130 losses due to combat engagements have been zero. It was a driving factor in the formal AMATS course being launched five years ago.

'Combat losses are not occurring due to enemy engagements, losses are occurring due to the misapplication of performance, energy management and crew resource management [CRM],' says Jaquish. 'In order to operate tactically, we must first operate safely.' While early training offerings from the 192nd included threat scenarios, the emphasis is now placed on properly executing standard Tactics, Techniques and Procedures (TTPs) in a performance-degraded environment, without the added stress of a threat scenario.

'We introduce TTPs in a building block approach in environmental conditions unique to Reno and unlike anything students have seen before. The first place to get introduced to

these conditions is not in combat, it is in the safe training environment that Reno provides,' says Jaquish. The 328th AS from Niagara Falls was the first unit to visit Reno for training in 2012. They came to Reno with three aircraft and four crews as part of their pre-deployment training. 'They came here for an Afghanistan deployment course,' says Jaquish. 'We had some threat reaction/avoidance as well with kill boxes to avoid. From that first iteration we started developing things and it matured into a tactics safety course. Now, the first class they receive — other than local familiarization — is about flying safety. What we teach is not about maximum performance in the mountains, it's about how to effectively and safely execute the TTPs.'

The rationale behind the seven-day course is that at some point a Hercules crew will be required to fly at low level — whether that's on departure from an airfield or arriving at a landing strip, a low-level air drop or avoiding ground threats. Explaining the threat mitigation element, Maj Jaquish says often just not being able to see the aircraft is sufficient. 'Flying low in terrain means the enemy only has visibility on the formation for

Left: **Learning how to manage the performance of the C-130 is what the AMATS course is all about. It tends to lead the 'High Rollers' instructors into some challenging terrain.**

Below: **'High Rollers' Hercs get down close to the granite as they hone their low-flying skills.**

a few seconds, which means there's not enough time for them to engage. There are a lot of advantages but also a lot of requirements to flying low. It's just going to happen in a Hercules.'

Lt Col Bravo adds: 'When you're in a threat environment you want to get down low and terrain mask. We teach the safe execution of flying low — down to 300ft above ground level [AGL] in the desert or 1,000ft AGL in a deep valley. You don't want turbulence to push you down into the terrain or if you have an engine shot out you have to be able to climb out. In a worst-case scenario a crew could be in a box canyon and

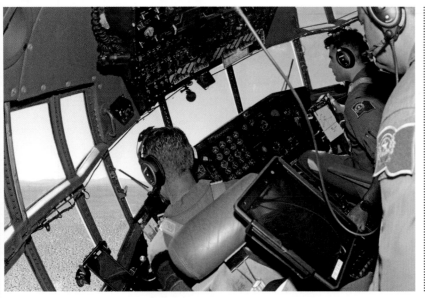

Above: **Flying into deep canyons means that pilots need to learn how to ensure they have a suitable escape out of the terrain. This 192nd AS C-130H is flying south along the deep Kern River Valley in the Sierra Nevada.**

Left: **The flight engineer in the C-130H is responsible for backing up the pilots — monitoring the radar altimeter and the performance of the engines.**

not have the performance to safely execute an escape. They have to respect the performance energy management required from the C-130 in austere low-performance conditions.'

The AMATS course is run in conjunction with the US Marine Corps' Mountain Warfare Training Center in Pickel Meadows, California. The 'High Rollers' deliver supplies to the Marines as part of the course and in return they run the mountain drop zones (DZs).

The AMATS course syllabus begins with a baseline building-block approach, but it can be tailored to the crew's experience levels. Coming from airfields and operating areas at near sea level, the altitudes and temperatures

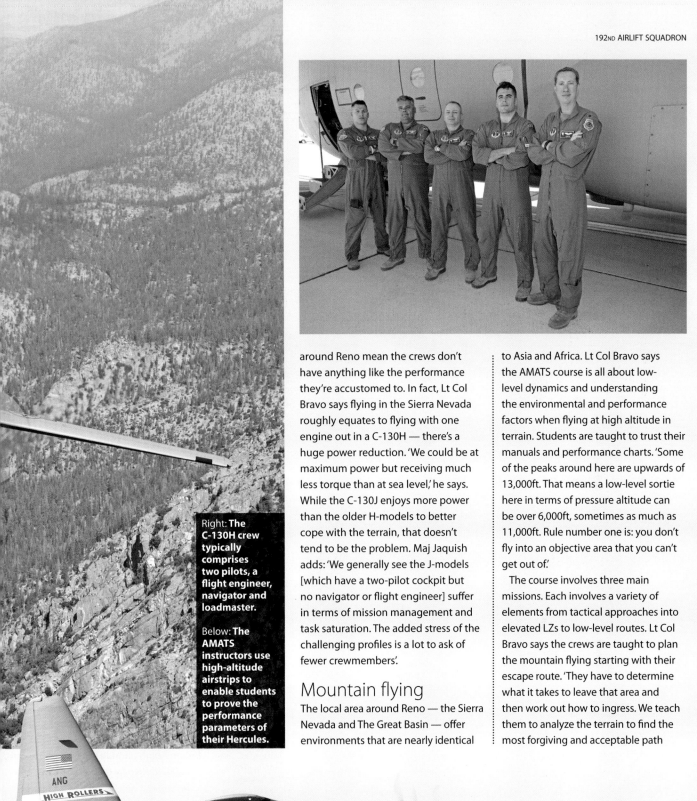

Right: **The C-130H crew typically comprises two pilots, a flight engineer, navigator and loadmaster.**

Below: **The AMATS instructors use high-altitude airstrips to enable students to prove the performance parameters of their Hercules.**

around Reno mean the crews don't have anything like the performance they're accustomed to. In fact, Lt Col Bravo says flying in the Sierra Nevada roughly equates to flying with one engine out in a C-130H — there's a huge power reduction. 'We could be at maximum power but receiving much less torque than at sea level,' he says. While the C-130J enjoys more power than the older H-models to better cope with the terrain, that doesn't tend to be the problem. Maj Jaquish adds: 'We generally see the J-models [which have a two-pilot cockpit but no navigator or flight engineer] suffer in terms of mission management and task saturation. The added stress of the challenging profiles is a lot to ask of fewer crewmembers'.

Mountain flying

The local area around Reno — the Sierra Nevada and The Great Basin — offer environments that are nearly identical

to Asia and Africa. Lt Col Bravo says the AMATS course is all about low-level dynamics and understanding the environmental and performance factors when flying at high altitude in terrain. Students are taught to trust their manuals and performance charts. 'Some of the peaks around here are upwards of 13,000ft. That means a low-level sortie here in terms of pressure altitude can be over 6,000ft, sometimes as much as 11,000ft. Rule number one is: you don't fly into an objective area that you can't get out of.'

The course involves three main missions. Each involves a variety of elements from tactical approaches into elevated LZs to low-level routes. Lt Col Bravo says the crews are taught to plan the mountain flying starting with their escape route. 'They have to determine what it takes to leave that area and then work out how to ingress. We teach them to analyze the terrain to find the most forgiving and acceptable path

ANG
HIGH ROLLERS
20554

U.S. AIR FORCE

NEVADA AIR GUARD

> 'Combat losses are not occurring due to enemy engagements, losses are occurring due to the misapplication of performance, energy management and crew resource management [CRM]'
>
> **Maj Joseph Jaquish**

and then determine their performance and climb gradient. The instructors actually do most of the routine mission planning. We plan the routes, the product development such as charts and checklists and we even do the mission briefing for them. We ask them to compute the performance data and then fly their numbers.'

The first mission involves a high-altitude decent into the pattern at the auxiliary landing field at Herlong, California. Bravo says: 'They fly assault patterns here and then they fly low level in the Sierra Nevada into steep canyons. On that first flight there is one heavy equipment airdrop and one container delivery system (CDS) airdrop. They also fly out over the high desert of The Great Basin, which means the 200ft trees that they saw in the Sierras are now 20ft bushes, so that visual disorientation

Above: **While the newer C-130Js enjoy more powerful engines and six-bladed propellers, older C-130Hs need to be carefully managed to ensure they have the requisite power to climb out of canyons and valleys.** Richard Collens

Left: **Maj Jaquish and 1st Lt Sperry at the controls of a 'High Rollers' C-130H3.**

teaches them how to not get too low.'

The second flight sees the start of work with the Marine Corps mountain warfare teams. The Hercules crews, usually operating as a pair, head to a drop zone that is 7,000ft above sea level as part of a hi-low-hi mission template. 'Firstly they have to plan their escape route out of what is a very big canyon,' says Bravo. 'They then have to work backwards, starting with their ingress from 11,000ft. It's a slow penetration to the airdrop, then a high-altitude escape up to about 12,000ft. They fly that profile twice and we find that the CRM aspects improve and things run much more efficiently on the second run.'

The final mission lasts for over three hours and is a capstone event. The visiting crews fly low-level routes in canyons, climb-outs over terrain, a short-notice on-call airdrop co-ordinated with Marine Corps Joint Terminal Attack Controllers (JTACs) and it culminates at the Sweetwater landing zone, which is a 3,500ft dirt strip at 6,800ft above mean sea level.

'After the crews complete day three at Sweetwater, I think any C-130 crew would be ready to fly any place in the world,' comments Lt Col Bravo.

'Sweetwater is just as challenging as anything we've seen in South-west Asia and Africa.'

The way the Air National Guard does business, with experienced crews remaining in one location for a significant period of their careers, lends itself perfectly to creating the kind of experience that is afforded by the 'High Rollers' — more than half of its crews are AMATS graduates. This can then be used to effectively impart this corporate knowledge to their peers. Units bring their own aircraft, but the Nevada ANG instructors ride along with them as they build their own experience. Lt Col Bravo says: 'They're not used to operating the aircraft in this demanding environment. This course is a safe place for the crews to learn and reduce mishaps.'

1st Lt Eric Sperry is one of the more junior pilots at the 192nd AS, but is already an AMATS graduate. 'The main things you learn as a student are performance and energy management. For the most part, C-130 units are located close to sea level in areas of temperate climate, in relatively flat areas. So on a day-to-day basis

Right: **A canyon wall flashes by. Terrain masking remains a vital tactic for C-130 crews in high-threat environments.**

Below: **No room for error. AMATS instructors strive to educate squadron pilots on the intricacies of flying the C-130 in challenging environments.**

aircraft performance may just be an afterthought. However, in a location such as Reno, where temperatures can vary from one extreme to the other, combined with the high elevation and mountainous terrain, make it the perfect area for crews to train in and mirror some of the most challenging environments to fly in the world.

'The course definitely reinforces our trust in 'the numbers'; the engineered

and charted performance data for the airplane. In fact, one of the academic sessions revolves solely around planning your own mission with your own calculations, then going out the next day and actually flying it as precisely as possible to demonstrate proof of concept. As a guy that flies on a regular basis at the unit where the course is offered, it provided me the opportunity to learn even more about mountain

Left, top to bottom: **The flying near Reno closely mirrors the terrain in Afghanistan and provides an ideal pre-deployment location.** Richard Collens

Loading a Modular Airborne Fire Fighting System (MAFFS II) for its delivery to the 152nd Airlift Wing in September 2016. ANG/1st Lt Monica Ebert

A 'High Rollers' C-130H dispenses water from the MAFFS II system during training. USAF/ TSgt Emerson Marcus

flying and sharpen my skills, in an area that I am familiar with. With that being said I can't imagine how valuable of a resource this course can be to other units who don't ever get to see this type of flying until they are in a deployed environment.'

Modular Airborne Fire Fighting System

With roughly 70 per cent of forest fires occurring within three hours flying time of Reno, the 'High Rollers' were an obvious choice to assume the MAFFS mission. The squadron's first crewmembers were formally trained in May 2016, and the wing was fully operational in June 2017. On July 22, 2017, the 'High Rollers' flew their first operational aircraft from the Fresno Air Attack Base in support of the US Forest Service (USFS), and continued to support firefighting efforts in California

for three months. 'This is the first time the Nevada Air Guard has been tasked as the active lead unit,' commented MSgt Jennifer Harrell, a 152nd AW crew chief. 'My tasking, as the crew chief, is to ensure the aircraft remains perfectly inspected and flyable and to co-ordinate any additional maintenance that may need to be performed,' she said. 'At the end of the day we recover the aircraft, do a full inspection, a rinse to ensure the retardant hasn't affected the aircraft and then we make sure the aircraft is ready for the next mission.'

Leading the MAFFS mission at Reno is Maj David McNally. 'This is the perfect mission for the Air National Guard because it means we can help our neighbors. We're working to have 10 full MAFFS crews and we have two MAFFS systems, which are actually owned by the Forest Service, so we have to be federally activated by them to load them up.'

Above: Hamilton Sundstrand composite eight-blade NP2000 propellers may be on the cards for the C-130H3 along with Rolls-Royce's Series 3.5 kits to enhance component performance.

The USFS typically turns to civilian air tankers before they call in the military. 'We offer a surge capability, filling the holes during the main fire season,' comments McNally. 'We were deployed to SoCal [southern California] for about three months this year.' He explains that this is a demanding mission and even the most seasoned pilots require around two years before they fly as the aircraft captain in the left seat. 'Our mountain flying helps us transition, but it takes a lot to get the full understanding of the Hercules when you're that heavy and flying up at 7,000ft fighting fires. MAFFS requires a lead [spotter] pilot who typically comes from the Bureau of Land Management, from Calfire or from the USFS. These are experienced tanker pilots that work with the ground incident commander and they lead us in 500ft formation. They pop smoke where they want us

to start deploying the retardant, with another puff of smoke to stop. They try to not put us in a bad situation as we are relying on them.'

The addition of this demanding role is an obvious progression for the men and women of the 'High Rollers'. There's a huge amount of experience in this famous unit, and it exemplifies the pinnacle of getting the most from the weary C-130Hs. As Maj McNally concludes: 'Bringing MAFFS to the 'High Rollers' made a lot of sense and it's very rewarding to have so many missions in a single Guard unit.'

Acknowledgments: **The author wishes to thank Col Anthony Machabee, Lt Col Todd Hudson, Lt Col David Chauvin, Lt Col Ricardo Bravo, Maj Joseph Jaquish, Maj David McNally, 1st Lt Eric Sperry and the crews of 'Roller' flight for their support of this feature.**

BAD GUYS
ON DEMAND

Although the US leads the field when it comes to Red Air aggressor units, it remains woefully short of what it requires to challenge its fifth-generation fighters. It's a problem that's being tackled via recruiting contractor air service providers on a huge scale.

report: **Jamie Hunter**

DESPITE EFFORTS TO recapitalize fighter fleets with the F-35A, the fact is that today's US Air Force has just 55 fighter squadrons. President Trump's plans to upscale aside, personnel levels are at an all-time low. The USAF says it is nearly 2,000 pilots short. Fewer squadrons mean more deployment rotations, and high airframe usage — the average age of its fighter aircraft is well over 30 years.

In 2014 the USAF was forced to cull one of its three aggressor squadrons to save money, but also to free up F-15Cs for Air National Guard squadrons. Today, the USAF's two remaining dedicated aggressor units — the 18th AGRS at Eielson AFB, Alaska, and the 64th AGRS at Nellis AFB, Nevada — are kept extremely active supporting 'Red Flag'

The 18th Aggressor Squadron at Eielson is mainly engaged in supporting the 'Red Flag — Alaska' series of exercises as well as the local F-22 Raptor units.
Jim Haseltine

and 'Red Flag — Alaska' exercises, as well as the Weapons School at Nellis, leaving little time for them to service front-line units. It means that regular Combat Air Force (CAF) squadrons have to turn their hand to flying as opponents in day-to-day training and in many exercises to supplement the full-time aggressor forces — everyone agrees that this is a poor use of such valuable assets.

Speaking earlier this year, Maj Gen Scott Vander Hamm, USAF Assistant Deputy Chief of Staff, Operations, told the *Yearbook*: 'Right now Air Combat Command is short by 28-40,000 sorties of Red Air, or Adversary Air [AdAir], each year.' He said the Air Force would like to cover this in house, but it can't. Therefore it's looking to farm out 'for a

short period of time' that service for contractors to provide the AdAir role.

F-22 Raptor pilots in particular have routinely raised concerns over flying against each other on a daily basis. Despite two Raptor wings having an aggressor T-38 Talon squadron to fight against as resident bad guys, they regularly fly against fellow Raptors that act as higher-end opponents. Former Air Combat Command (ACC) boss Gen Herbert 'Hawk' Carlisle said in 2016 that pitting fifth-generation F-22s and F-35s against each other amounted to 'zero training and almost negative training'. He added: 'generating our own adversary from fifth generation is counter-productive' — he said it's a draw on the airframe plus it doesn't present great training.

USAF

To challenge the crews, former aggressor pilot Carlisle said (before he retired) that F-22 and F-35 pilots needed to train against an effective aggressor force that outnumbered them by a factor of 3:1 or 4:1.

While the T-38 aggressors embedded alongside F-22 squadrons offer those numbers, the only real advantage the Talon pilot has is a small visual signature. F-22 pilots need to go up against a radar-equipped adversary and for the

Left top to bottom: **An aggressor F-16C takes on fuel from a KC-135R. Despite talk of a new USAF aggressor squadron, the manning crisis may preclude this.** USAF/ SSgt Maeson L. Elleman

The T-38 Talons of the 2nd Fighter Squadron, co-located at Tyndall, provide the majority of the Red Air aggressor training for Raptor students. USAF/ MSgt Burt Traynor

'BVR [beyond visual range] is where the adversary requirement is the highest, and contracted Red Air needs to, and is starting to, bring forward a more sophisticated adversary with a radar and a jammer'

Red Air to be able to hold its own in the visual fight.

It's not just the USAF. A senior Marine Corps officer told this magazine: 'It's challenging to generate the level of Red Air the [F-35] requires. BVR [beyond visual range] is where the adversary requirement is the highest, and contracted Red Air needs to, and is starting to, bring forward a more sophisticated adversary with a radar and a jammer — that's what we really need. We simply require large numbers of adversaries to challenge us.'

The requirement

ACC is looking to place an effective, resident aggressor squadron at each of its fifth-generation fighter bases. In the case of the 1st Fighter Wing at Joint Base Langley-Eustis, the 71st Fighter Training Squadron 'Ironmen' provides daily support to the resident Raptor squadrons. 'When both squadrons are in town, we generally provide four T-38s for each, and they add between two and four Red Air Raptors to go up against the four Blue Force Raptors,' commented one T-38 pilot. 'For us, a lot of it is about strength in numbers; they kill us, we die and regenerate and be alive again. They will have certain DLOs [Desired Learning Objectives] to achieve on each mission and it's our job to set a presentation or tactic that drives those DLOs. For example, if we get to within visual range, if we can pick a Raptor up visually, that would be a DLO for them. They might be looking to fight a bandit that has a presentation in azimuth, maybe in a super-wide lane, or in range, so we present different pictures to drive those objectives. If we get to the merge we have met their DLO, because in general their tactics rely on them not being seen. We don't fly BFM [basic fighter maneuvers] with the Raptors, because they outperform us. Their learning objective was 30 seconds to a minute before that — their decision that got them into that merge.'

Bereft of any advanced sensors or weapons, the T-38 pilots have to get creative when it comes to simulating a credible threat. 'We know the ranges and angles we need to simulate the WEZ [weapon engagement zone] of the weapon we are replicating,' commented a pilot.

The expanding F-35A community needs similar aggressor support squadrons and many believe ACC will

grow its Talon aggressor business as the new T-X trainer comes online and frees up T-38Cs, which may be available as active-duty or government-furnished equipment in the hands of contractors.

While there is talk of standing up a third aggressor squadron there is a huge requirement for contractor support to supplement the in-house Red Air for the next 15 to 20 years. 'We need capacity and the threat is getting better, the density and the environment is getting more challenging, so we need it more than we used to need it,' Carlisle said.

Despite the emphasis that is put upon live flying, the USAF is also hard at work developing its live, virtual, constructive (LVC) training to make full use of sensors and capabilities in a secure environment — testing pilots in a high-end series of scenarios in a simulator, away from

prying eyes. Despite such advances, the need to maintain effective live flying remains.

The long-term situation regarding contractor support for the USAF is unclear and some say this is a short-term sticking plaster to fix an urgent requirement. The USAF ultimately aspires to hold a competition out past 2025 that will lead to the procurement of an 'AdAir-X' aggressor aircraft to replace the current fleet of 36 aggressor F-16s, the contracted Red Air and the adversary T-38s. Some say a tailored version of the new T-X aircraft will fill this requirement and that this was a driving factor in the high-performance criteria laid out in T-X.

The USAF plan

In July 2016, the USAF issued a request for information for the AdAir capability

Left: **Draken dispatched four L-159E 'Honey Badgers' to Europe this summer to participate in the Fighter Weapons Instructor Training (FWIT) program. USAF training with the L-159s began in late April 2017 with adversary missions supporting the Weapons School at Nellis.**
Frank Crébas

Below: **Former RNZAF A-4K serial N146EM on the flightline at Edwards during F-35 support.**
Frank Crébas

— reaching out to the various contractor air service companies to support this massive emerging training need. The solicitation to industry was for nearly 42,000 hours of contracted aggressor support training at 12 different bases. As well as at Nellis AFB, other installations on the list comprised Seymour Johnson AFB, North Carolina; JB Pearl Harbor-Hickam, Hawaii; Holloman AFB, New Mexico; Eglin AFB, Florida; JB Langley-Eustis, Virginia; Tyndall AFB, Florida; Kingsley Field, Oregon; Luke AFB, Arizona; Hill AFB, Utah and Tucson Airport, Arizona. Nellis alone will take 11,250 hours of the requested flight hours annually. The service reportedly suffered from a shortage of adversary 3,000 sorties at Nellis during 2016 and that number is expected to rise as F-35 training ramps up.

This 2016 shortfall triggered a year-long experiment at the Nevada base for Draken International, one such supplier of contracted aggressor services. The contractor placed A-4 Skyhawks at Nellis to support both Weapons School and exercise training, working in concert with the resident 64th Aggressor Squadron and the 57th Adversary Tactics Group. It underscored how the use of contractor owned, contractor operated (COCO) adversary aircraft has been building for several years.

The USAF awarded a one-year contract to Draken. During the 'proof-of-concept' evaluation the company's radar-

equipped A-4K Skyhawks have been flying sorties from Nellis in support of the USAF Weapons School and the F-35 Joint Operational Test Team. It's a contract that proved so successful that Draken received an extension to the deal and it has also expanded its presence with the deployment of its new Aero Vodochody L-159 'Honey Badgers'.

The solution

The larger multi-award contract, which is now expected in mid-2019, recognizes how a single contractor cannot hope to possess the mass and footprint to win

outright — this is most likely going to be shared between the various big players in the market. Not only must these AdAir contractors meet the scale of the requirement in terms of locations and numbers of assets, but they must also present aircraft with the requisite mission sets. The USAF RFI lays the groundwork for a supersonic aircraft equipped with radar plus sensor and datalink capabilities.

Draken International has gained something of a lead thanks to its Nellis experiment. It has also supported Royal Netherlands Air Force F-35 testing out of Edwards AFB. The US Navy has been far

more forward leaning than the USAF when it comes to using contracted aggressors. The Textron-owned Airborne Tactical Advantage Company (ATAC) has performed tactical flight training for over 20 years, mainly servicing the Navy Fleet Replenishment Squadrons (FRS) and TOPGUN, providing Hawker Hunters and IAI Kfirs in the air-to-air role, as well as in electronic warfare and electronic threat replication. ATAC says this has provided 'tens of millions of dollars in savings for US taxpayers, reduced wear and tear on US military aircraft, and a consistently noted increase in military readiness for US forces worldwide.'

Above: **An ATAC Kfir formates on a VFC-13 F-5N during a mission supporting TOPGUN at NAS Fallon.** Rob 'Nuts' DeStasio

Below: **A Kfir, operated by ATAC, returns to NAS Fallon having supported an Air Wing Fallon exercise mission.** Rich Cooper

The likes of ATAC jets are manned by highly experienced pilots, many of whom have retired from military flying as TOPGUN or Weapons School patch wearers. They provide a pool of ideal talent with which to help train new aviators. Matt 'Race' Bannon of ATAC is a retired TOPGUN graduate. He says: 'The Navy has training shortfalls everywhere and they figure out how to best use ATAC. For example, FRS training. The FRS squadrons have so many sorties to fly and limited resources, so they in particular have identified huge value in contract air services. That training is always local, and using their own FRS assets to fly as adversaries increases their sortie count by at least twofold.' It is interesting to note that the majority of early FRS adversary training requires fairly benign setups, and can easily be achieved using a platform such as the Kfir that offers far lower running costs over a front-line Super Hornet, for example. Bannon adds: 'I'm not an Su-30 'Flanker' flying up at 40,000ft trying to kill their fighters. I'm more of a MiG-21 on a DLI (deck-launched intercept). If you ask a fighter pilot what they want I'm sure they'd say a Su-30 or similar, but that's going to cost you a lot of money, so that model sees the value of using a contractor air service being eroded.'

High end

It's at the higher end that the current USAF requirement appears to sit. Tactical Air Support (TacAir) of Reno, Nevada, has acquired a fleet of 21 F-5E/Fs from the Royal Jordanian Air Force, which will make it the world's largest private operator of the Northrop fighter. TacAir already operates five ex-Royal Canadian Air Force CF-5D Freedom Fighters and previously acquired Canada's entire inventory of spare parts including 65 General Electric J85 turbojet engines.

The contractor expects the fighters to begin supporting the US Department of Defense in early 2017 once they have undergone work at TacAir's maintenance and logistics facility in St Augustine, Florida. This is likely to be offered mainly to the US Navy initially. TacAir says the beauty of the F-5 is that it has a proven track record in the adversary field and that there are a number of specific upgrades that can be used to enhance these fighters.

Draken International continues to support USAF training efforts under the service's current pathfinder contract.

Draken's A-4K Skyhawks have supported Dutch F-35A operational test work at Edwards AFB, California.
Frank Crébas

Three Draken International L-159E 'Honey Badgers' fly near Holloman in September.
Draken International/Erik Hildebrandt

Discovery A-4s work closely with Wittmund's Eurofighters. In the hands of an experienced operator, the A-4 provides a very capable adversary platform for a sensible running cost.
Rich Cooper

That support is still provided by the ex-Royal New Zealand Air Force A-4Ks and L-159s. In addition, Draken owns a fleet of Aermacchi MB339CBs and little-used MiG-21s. The A-4Ks proved to be an important step in developing the company, with the aircraft acquired from New Zealand in 2012. This comprised nearly the full fleet of RNZAF Skyhawks that became surplus after the type's retirement. 'We specifically purchased jets that are rich in modern capabilities. In the case of our A-4K Skyhawks, they are equipped with the AN/APG-66 radar, AN/ALR-66 radar warning receiver, countermeasures, electronic attack pods, head-up display, hands on throttle and stick (HOTAS) controls, MFD and a 1553 databus. For all purposes, our A-4Ks are outfitted similarly to an F-16A but at dramatically lower operating costs', explained Draken boss Jared Isaacman. 'We also purchased 21 L-159E fighter jets. The L-159E is equipped with the Selex Grifo-L radar and attack software suite. They are a modern, virtually brand-new fourth-generation

fighter aircraft with extremely low operational costs. In both cases, the A-4 and L-159 enable Draken to provide tactically relevant adversary support but at dramatically lower costs than a comparable military F-16 or F-15 fighter.'

The pilot roster at Draken is equally impressive and includes top names in the industry, like Lt Col Jerry 'Jive' Kerby (ret.) and CAPT Dale 'Snort' Snodgrass (ret.). The company has also deployed aircraft to Europe and has taken part in large-force training exercises in support of the Japan Self-Defense Force at White Sands Missile Range, New Mexico. Draken deployed 18 aircraft to Holloman AFB from September 9-17, 2016, for the exercise. 'This exercise demonstrated Draken's enormous capacity to meet and exceed growing requirements within this unique industry. We see our fleet of fighter aircraft not just as credible and affordable platforms, but as a continuously expanding array of threat-representative capabilities', says Sean Gustafson, Draken's Vice President of Business Development. He adds: 'We

Left: **USAF aggressor assets like this F-16C from the 18th AGRS will be supplemented by the new AdAir contract.** Jim Haseltine

This image: **TacAir has released this image of one of its recently acquired former Royal Jordanian Air Force F-5s.** TacAir

will continue to modernize to ensure our fleet meets the training requirements of the future. This includes new technology such as passive infra-red sensors, AESA radars, helmet-cueing systems and an open-architecture datalink network.'

Indeed, Draken completed the purchase of 22 former Spanish Mirage F1M and F1B fighters in 2017 to take its fleet to over 100 aircraft. It will not only allow Draken to better service the USAF requirement but it also says the Naval Aviation Warfighting Development Center (NAWDC) at NAS Fallon, Nevada, is reviewing proposals from contract air service providers for a high-end supersonic, radar-equipped adversary solution. The contractor expects to equip the F1s with a helmet-mounted cueing system, infra-red missile seekers, datalinks, and electronic jamming and radar warning receiver capabilities.

Long-term Navy support operation ATAC has also been shopping for redundant Mirage F1s. It has purchased 63 Mirage F1s from France along with support equipment and 150 engines. Textron, the owner of ATAC, plans to offer the Mirages in relation to the USAF requirement and is planning to retrofit around 45 of the F1s with modern avionics systems such as digital radio-frequency memory-jamming capabilities and upgraded radars.

Known as Top Aces in the US market, Discovery Air Defence Services was able to take advantage of a highly proactive Canadian stance when it came to training and in 2005 won a contract to provide the Canadian Forces with aggressor training. It has recently renewed that contract for a further 10 years. The company acquired its A-4N Skyhawks through the takeover of Advanced Training Systems International (ATSI) of Mesa, Arizona, in December

Above: **Kfirs from ATAC provide assets to supplement resident adversaries during periods of peak operations.**
Rich Cooper

Below: **ATAC has acquired ex-French Air Force Mirage F1s including CR and CT variants.**
Jamie Hunter

2013. These ex-Israeli Air Force jets joined a fleet of ex-Luftwaffe Alpha Jets in the training arena, and highlighted the company's ambition to make a footprint into Europe.

While Discovery continues its work in Germany under the gaze of other European nations, its strategic approach means it is also looking to the future. It is set to acquire F-16 Fighting Falcons from

desert storage with the knowledge of the benefits such a platform would bring fourth- and fifth-generation fighter pilot training.

Overall, the requirement across the US Department of Defense has resulted in a huge upsurge in the contractor air services market. Whilst this is designed to help relieve the burden and wear on USAF squadrons, a negative downside is

almost certainly going to be that more experienced active-duty pilots walk out of the door and into some of these contractor jobs. In October 2017, it appeared that the final USAF RFP, which had been expected in late 2017, had slipped to April 2018. A contract award is now anticipated in May 2019, with flight operations starting in June 2019.

A pair of Boeing B-1B
Lancers — one each from
the 28th Bomb Wing's 37th
Bomb Squadron (BS) 'Tigers'
and 34th BS 'T-Birds' — flies
past the majestic Mount
Rushmore, South Dakota.

The US Air Force's B-1B Lancer fleet has seen many
changes, notably its adaptation to the conventional
role and its transfer to Air Force Global Strike Command.
Through all of this, the units that form part of the 28th
Bomb Wing at Ellsworth AFB, South Dakota, have
remained heavily committed to the front line.

report and photos: **Ted Carlson/Fotodynamics**

WHILE THEY MAY be 1980s-vintage aircraft, the US Air Force's Rockwell B-1B Lancers remain viable and lethal assets in today's sophisticated war-fighting arena. While the 'Bone' no longer has a nuclear role, as a result of an arms treaty with Russia, the aircraft possesses an outstanding low-level capability and can also deliver the goods from high altitude at stand-off distances, while sometimes being called upon simply to perform a non-kinetic 'show of force' to deter foes. This has been demonstrated during the type's use in conflicts on a fairly regular basis since 2001.

Having previously been Air Combat Command assets, the Lancers now fall under the Air Force Global Strike Command (AFGSC) umbrella. Prior to the realignment, the nuclear-capable bombers were already part of AFGSC, and it was deemed to be more efficient to have such aircraft reporting and being aligned to a single, centrally managed parent organization, regardless of whether they have a nuclear capability or not. The B-1, B-2, and B-52 all have functional strengths and weaknesses, so employment can be custom-tailored to fit the mission at hand.

One of the latest B-1B modifications is Sustainment Block 16 (SB16). This is a robust upgrade that includes new avionics, adds multi-function displays and enhances the jet's Link 16 capability. It makes the crew's job much easier, allowing them to focus on more important events during a mission and avoiding the potential for task saturation. Sensors have become an instrumental component of the Lancer's

LANCER FORCE

armory, the latest version of the Sniper ATP (Advanced Targeting Pod) being the ATP-SE (Sensor Enhancement) variant. With these upgrades, both squadrons at Ellsworth Air Force Base, South Dakota, stand ready to deploy on a moment's notice.

'Bone' drivers

Ellsworth AFB is home to the 28th Bomb Wing, consisting of two operational combat B-1B squadrons: the 34th Bomb Squadron (BS) 'Thunderbirds' and the 37th BS 'Tigers'. 'The B-1 is a great asset to fly due to being both 'crew-based' and a large, powerful jet', commented Capt David, a pilot with the 37th BS who has 800 hours of Lancer flight time and has been stationed at Ellsworth for the past three years. 'It goes very low and very fast', he says, 'plus it has quite good maneuverability for such a large aircraft. It is a fairly simple jet to fly and a lot of fun.'

The crew consists of four — a pilot, co-pilot, and two WSOs (weapon systems operators) situated aft of the pilots. The defensive systems officer resides on the left-hand side, while the offensive

systems officer mans the right. 'Some flights I may be the mission lead', David continues, 'and other flights the WSO may do it — we rotate.

'Recently I have been in two different theaters of operation for combat. In the South-west Asia CENTCOM [US Central Command] area, we often integrated into large joint-service and country formations, with over 50 aircraft involved. We all had the same mindset and mission goals on who we were targeting. A single flight could last anywhere from 10 to 20 hours. We would need tanker support, and one mission our formation of aircraft employed over 150 weapons. France and the Netherlands both participated and were heavily involved in that mission.

'[In] another operating area in a different direction, we were supporting special tactics personnel via close air support [CAS], and we had the opportunity to meet them in person as they would flow through the base. It was great to be able to support those guys and their fight. They were able to regain territory they had lost; we could see the

Left: A fabulous top view of a B-1B with wings swept fully back to 67 degrees.

Above: **Two pilots in a B-1B with a Sustainment Block 16 cockpit run through pre-start checks. Note that the crews tend to wear headsets during their pre-flight tasks, switching to helmets for the actual flight.**

progress and that we were helping to make a difference.'

'I truly enjoy the crew make-up of four tactically proficient, smart aviators all working together to solve problems within one jet', added Lt Col Seth Spanier, the commander of the 34th BS. He has 2,700 hours in the B-1, 1,300 of which having been notched up in combat. He served with the 37th BS from 2004-11, and made four deployments. The first was to Guam, and the last three all to the Middle East. Spanier was a B-1 weapons school instructor and later chief of operations for Pacific Air Forces, managing the continuous bomber presence at Guam. He took command of the 'T-Birds' in June 2016, and the unit soon thereafter deployed to Guam.

Spanier continued: 'The aircraft itself is flexible, capable, and an impressive machine. It is like flying three different airplanes, one being high-altitude cruise with the wings forward, [another] low-altitude with the wings fully aft, and lastly in the traffic pattern low and slow, with the wings forward. A pilot has to

learn how to fly the 'Bone' in all three flight regimes. The new SB16 upgrade is amazing, and it is easy to be good in an SB16 jet — it is the new B-1 of today. Going from the SB15 to the SB16 was a huge leap, and mastering the B-1 happens much sooner. I love the power, the maneuverability, and it is a great airplane to fly.

'In the past 10 years, we have gone through constant software block upgrades and each version was an evolutionary step. We adopted the Sniper targeting pod in 2008; that exponentially increased our capability with electro-optical targeting solutions and allowed us to better fly the CAS role. Also included are flying IMC [in instrument conditions] and through clouds, and the pod gives us good accuracy. That being said, the SB16 was a revolutionary upgrade, compared to all evolutionary upgrades before. While the airplane still performs the same, the increased ability allowing the crew to interface with the jet, along with datalink sharing with other platforms, makes crew synergies extremely easy and frees us all up, minimizing task saturation.

'We currently are using the Sniper SE pod… We started with the Sniper XL,

Above: With Ellsworth AFB in the background, resident 'Bones' head out for a mission.

followed by the AT, and the ATs were modified into the current SEs that enhance our maritime mode, along with increased sensor fidelity and better target resolution. A couple of our newer weapons include the AGM-158B JASSM-ER [Joint Air-to-Surface Standoff Missile — Extended Range], with the ability to carry 24 on one aircraft, and the very capable 500lb GBU-54 LJDAM [Laser JDAM]. We can now hit fast-moving and maneuvering ground targets. For the maritime role, we soon will have guided mines. Essentially we add a JDAM tail kit to the normally unguided Quickstrike series of mine, calling them the Quickstrike-J.

'The next B-1 upgrade will be SB17, which will enhance the machine-to-machine interface; the Sniper pod will be more fully integrated into the [avionics software], and the anti-ship AGM-158C LRASM [Long-Range Anti-Ship Missile] will be fully integrated. Other future upgrades will be a helmet-mounted cueing system that will interface with Sniper and the other sensors on the jet. Later, a new BRU-56 bomb rack will allow us to carry the Small Diameter Bomb, and have two 500lb weapons per station, allowing for a total of 48. Another important long-term B-1 upgrade will be the defensive avionics enhancements.

'We just returned from a CBP [Continuous Bomber Presence] deployment at Guam. It is a PACOM [US Pacific Command] mission and we work for PACAF while in theater, rotating within the theater as the commander sees fit. The point of it is assurance and deterrence; essentially we assure our allies, and deter our potential adversaries. Terms such as long-range and Pacific power projection are officially used too, but we simply call them higher-headquarters missions because that is where they are directed from. A typical mission involves taking off and joining up with a tanker, then traveling to some far-reaching portion of the Pacific.

'During our deployment, we were as far west as Diego Garcia, we went to the eastern seaboard, as far north as Alaska, and down south to the lower part of Australia. It is a massive area. We made multiple penetrations into the South China Sea, and worked around the Korean area. It gave our crews the opportunity to perform a whole spectrum of new and different B-1 mission sets, and work within a new-to-us AOR [area of responsibility]. The training was invaluable. We saw some pretty impressive results from our crews

Above: **Part of the impressive flight line at Ellsworth AFB.**

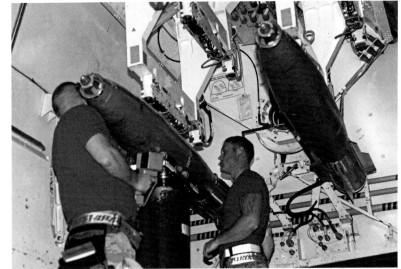

Right top to bottom: **Maintainers load 500lb iron bombs into one of the B-1's three cavernous weapons bays.**

The Sniper Advanced Targeting Pod (ATP) has dramatically improved the B-1's versatility.

Above: **The B-1B's three weapons bays can accommodate a wide variety of weapons and configurations — making this a superbly versatile platform.**

Right: **A B-1 Lancer crew with aircraft serial 86-0099 *Ruptured Duck* of the 28th BW.**

Left: **The Weapons Systems Officer stations in the back of the B-1B complete with the latest Sustainment Block 16 cockpit upgrades.**

and it was helpful working alongside of our allies.'

Changing times

'The B-1 has come a long way during my time in the aircraft, since I first came to it back in 1997', said Col John Martin, the 28th BW operations group commander. He has 2,500 B-1B flight hours, four combat deployments and is a recipient of the Gen Curtis E. LeMay Award for the best overall bomber crew in the Air Force and the Bronze Star. He initially served with the 37th BS, then the 28th Operations Support Squadron; he was an instructor at Dyess AFB, Texas with the 28th BS, and later he was the 34th BS commander.

'While I was at the schoolhouse squadron in 1997', Martin went on, 'it

was then when we stopped performing the nuclear role in the B-1, on October 1 of that year. The aircraft had originally been designed to penetrate Russia during the Cold War and we had a nuclear-only mission. That was why the B-1 didn't participate in 'Desert Storm'. The decision was made to upgrade the aircraft to what they called the CMUP [Conventional Munitions Upgrade Program].

'Initially we dropped a lot of 500lb Mk82 general-purpose unguided bombs. A few years later, the 2,000lb GBU-31 JDAM materialized and became the go-to weapon. The 500lb GBU-38 followed. The JDAMs are frequently our weapons of choice and have been used around the world by B-1s, including in Afghanistan, Syria, and Iraq. Just a couple of years ago we started using the GBU-54 Laser JDAM, and that works well in conjunction with our Sniper pod.

'Sustainment Block 16 doesn't change what we do or the munitions we carry. It changes how we do things and interact with the aircraft. It expedites the kill chain for us and turns the B-1 into a millennial jet; it now is a hybrid 'glass' cockpit with color MFDs [multi-function displays], and is more computer-oriented with mice and cursors. You can right-click on a target and simply select which weapon you wish to employ against the target. It is well-suited and intuitive for our younger generation that has grown up with this technology.

'The 34th BS just returned from our first Continuous Bomber Presence, [something] we haven't executed in the past 10 years in the B-1 community. We

have been very busy in other theaters, mostly Afghanistan, so only the B-2s and B-52s had been supporting the CBP. The 34th flew in a major Pacific theater exercise called 'Valiant Shield'. As for real-time events [during] that deployment, after North Korea set off a nuclear bomb we flew a deterrence mission along the DMZ [demilitarized zone] and landed the jet at Osan for their airshow.

'From July 2015 through January 2016, the 37th RS deployed to the desert and set a record for the highest number of weapons dropped in theater — 5,037 to be exact — and it was very 'kinetically engaged' with the foes in Iraq, Syria, and a lesser amount in Afghanistan. Most missions, they returned 'Winchester' — all ordnance expended. Some missions, they were tasked to drop on financial

Above: A B-1B down low and fast on a mission from Ellsworth.

Below: As night falls at Ellsworth the B-1 night shift comes online. Set against a full moon, the four General Electric F101 engines crackle into reheat.

banks, disrupting the ISIS cashflow, crippling their monetary supply line.

'As for the wing challenges, manning is the biggest hurdle. There is an acute rated-aviator shortage across the entire Air Force, and we are well short of the number of crews we would like to have. We have been on a constant 'snappy ops tempo' since 2006 and that creates a drain on manpower. The old saying that you can do more with less can only go on for so long, and sequestration has not helped.

'I am hopeful and optimistic the new administration will help us turn the situation around, not only with manning, but to get the tools and parts we need, ultimately increasing our readiness. Both squadrons have been doing tremendous work, especially

with the limited resources we now have. Since October 2001, we have essentially been in non-stop combat operations in a variety of places. However, it has impacted our readiness rate some. We have been a workhorse in OEF [Operation 'Enduring Freedom'], OIR [Operation 'Iraqi Freedom'], OFS [Operation 'Freedom's Sentinel'], throughout South-west Asia, and earners in the war on terrorism since 2001.'

The commander of the 28th BW is Brig Gen (Sel) Gentry Boswell, who has amassed more than 5,000 flight hours. He initially flew in intelligence and reconnaissance aircraft, including the RC-135S/U/V/W, command and control missions in US Navy E-6Bs, and then electronic warfare tasks in B-1Bs. Boswell

Above: **A great shot showing off the side and underside views of the B-1B.**

Below: **A 'Bone' bangs down at Ellsworth after a mission to the local ranges.**

started training on the Lancer in 1999. He has served with all three current operational 'Bone' squadrons over the years, those being the Dyess-based 9th BS 'Bats' as well as the 34th and 37th BS. 'Since I joined the community', he says, 'it has been a steady stream of combat operations. In the first three years with B-1s, I deployed three times, which included the Pacific, European, and the Middle East theaters.

'The airmen that employ and maintain the B-1 truly drive the innovation that has continually changed the aircraft into the premier battlefield instrument of today. That includes payload, range, and speed to do a variety of things, [those] being the aircraft's best attributes. Gen Mosley [the former USAF chief of staff] has called the B-1 the 'roving linebacker' — that relates to a football field, being able to cover any threat and deal with it, having great range, precision, and speed.

'When I first came into the B-1 community, we could put a 2,000lb bomb into your back yard at 10

miles away. Today, we can take that same bomb and put it through your doorknob at twice the distance. The sensor integration with the Sniper pod has been a huge leap forward for us. We are one of the few platforms that can organically initiate and complete a kill chain. The non-kinetic capabilities are great also. Using the pod, we can perform surveillance and reconnaissance, with the ability to simply monitor and watch. Then as events develop, the B-1 can go right into a kinetic engagement.

'With SB16, we now have the ability to take all of the information from a great variety of assets on the battlefield and pump it into the cockpit through the datalink. Then we marry that with the kinetic systems on the aircraft, and we have a God's eye view of the battlefield with great situational awareness. That will keep us on the cutting edge — lethal, capable, and precise — over the next 10 to 15 years. Bombers all have persistence, payload, and now precision,

and that keeps us relevant. The mitigating factor we will always need to balance in the future is survivability, and the B-1's low-level and high-speed capability, coupled with its impressive defensive avionics suite and stand-off weapon arsenal, afford it excellent survivability.

'Here at home, the Powder River Training Complex was just enlarged, so we now have the largest slice of military training airspace in the nation; it is even larger than the Nellis range. We conduct large-force exercises in it four times per year. Recently we have shifted over to the Pacific and European theaters and that has brought value to us in the community. We were in the CENTCOM area for the past decade, so it is a moderate shift for us because we have been in that mindset for a while now. We will deploy all over the world, wherever our leadership needs us to be, and that gives us a global perspective.'

Acknowledgments: **Thanks to Brig Gen (Sel) Gentry Boswell (commander, 28th BW), Col John Martin (commander, 28th OG), Lt Col Seth 'Cocker' Spanier (commander, 34th BS), Capt Michael (37th BS pilot), Steven Merrill, 2nd Lt Miranda (chief, 28th BW public affairs), SSgt Hailey Staker (28th BW/PA), David Garrett (28th OSS), and the many other members of the 28th BW who helped, together with Capts Richard and Dan of the 509th BW/394th CTS.**

A pair of B-1B Lancers of the 28th BW flies past the spectacular Devil's Tower National Monument in Wyoming.

"*The aircraft itself is flexible, capable, and an impressive machine. It is like flying three different airplanes, one being high-altitude cruise with the wings forward, [another] low-altitude with the wings fully aft, and lastly in the traffic pattern low and slow, with the wings forward*'
Lt Col Seth Spanier

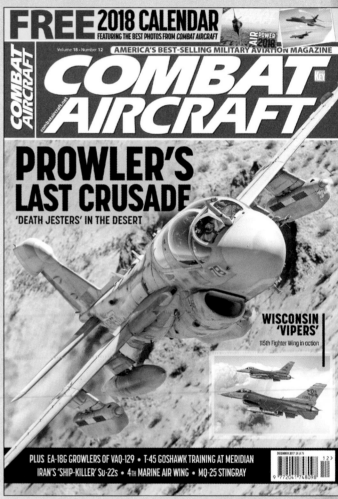

LIGHTNING'S
GLOBAL PRESENCE

Having marked initial operating capability in 2016, the F-35As of Hill AFB have been making their presence known on the world stage via two high-profile deployments.

report: **Jamie Hunter**

WHEN A PAIR of F-35As touched down at Kadena Air Base, Okinawa, Japan on October 31 it marked the start of the most significant event to date for the US Air Force Lightning II. It was the start of a 12-aircraft, six-month deployment to the Pacific, a region that has never been far from the headlines in recent times.

No doubt a show of force to North Korea and a sign of US strength and commitment to the region — these are busy times for the men and women of the USAF's first operational F-35 unit. Having declared initial operating capability in 2016, the pace of life for the USAF's lead warfighting Lightning II unit is unrelenting.

Deploying as part of a new Pacific Air Forces (PACAF) Theater Security Program (TSP), Hill AFB's Lightnings carry the 'HL' tail code of the Utah installation and are led by the 34th Fighter Squadron 'Rams'. However, the 12 aircraft are jointly operated by the active-duty 388th Fighter Wing and the Air Force Reserve Command's 419th Fighter Wing.

The USAF said the deployment was designed to 'demonstrate the continuing US commitment to stability and security in the region' — with 300 airmen heading west from Hill AFB, this is a major effort.

The F-35As of Hill AFB have rarely been out of the headlines this year. Even Stateside, they've been on the road to a number of bases on smaller-scale training detachments.
USAF/ Michael McCool

The initial two aircraft arrived ahead of the main party having participated in the Seoul Aerospace and Defense Exhibition. The balance of 10 jets were in place at Kadena by November 2, poised to begin flight operations alongside the assets of the resident 18th Wing, including two active-duty F-15C squadrons. 'The F-35A gives the joint warfighter unprecedented global precision attack capability against current and emerging threats while complementing our air superiority fleet,' commented Gen Terrence J. O'Shaughnessy, Pacific Air Forces commander. 'The airframe is ideally suited to meet our command's obligations, and we look forward to integrating it into our training and operations.'

Deployment debut

The six-month Kadena deployment came on the back of a period spent in the UK at RAF Lakenheath in April. Six jets arrived at the Suffolk base with little warning, but to huge fanfare on April 15, followed by a further pair four days later. This move east was supported by a C-5 and C-17s to bring in roughly 200 airmen and their kit from Hill. The 'Rams' detachment set up shop alongside the resident 493rd FS 'Grim Reapers' F-15C/D unit — flying local missions alongside their hosts.

When the Hill jets touched down in the UK it marked the start of the USAF's first overseas training deployment to Europe with the F-35A. Luke AFB F-35s from the 56th FW attended the Royal International

Air Tattoo in 2016, but they came only for airshow purposes. The Lakenheath visit was undoubtedly the precursor to the larger and longer deployment to Japan in what has turned out to be an incredibly busy year for the Hill personnel. The USAF is truly putting its latest fighters to work.

The Lakenheath deployment was all about proving capability through the chance to come as a complete squadron and fly operationally representative training missions. Plus, the choice of the UK base was no coincidence — the resident 48th FW is planned as the first overseas basing location for USAF Lightning IIs.

Once bedded down at Lakenheath, the F-35s embarked on a range

Above: **An F-35A arrives at Kadena, Okinawa, Japan, on November 2, having flown from Joint Base Hickam, Hawaii.** USAF/SrA Omari Bernard

Below: **Lt Col Michael Albrecht, 388th Operations Support Squadron director of operations, shakes hands with Lt Col Matthew Johnston, 34th FS commander, after arriving at Kadena.** USAF/SSgt Benjamin Sutton

Above: **A pair of Hill F-35As ensconced in the concrete shelter at Kadena. Their arrival here marked the F-35A's first deployment to the Indo-Asia-Pacific region.** USAF/SrA Quay Drawdy

Below: **The 34th FS has been flying missions alongside the resident F-15Cs of the 44th and 67th FS.** USAF/SrA Omari Bernard

of training operations under the European Reassurance Initiative, a series of exercises and training opportunities with NATO allies meant to signal strength to Russia and improve interoperability. Pairs of F-35s also forward deployed to Estonia and Bulgaria to 'maximize training opportunities, build partnerships with allied air forces, and become familiar with Europe's diverse operating conditions', according to a statement.

Two F-35As accompanied by about 20 supporting airmen flew to Ämari air base, Estonia, for the day on April 25 for 'familiarization training'. A statement said: 'the deployment has been planned for some time, has no relations to

current events and was conducted in close co-ordination with Estonian allies.'

A second 'out and back' flight was conducted to Graf Ignatievo air base, Bulgaria, on April 28, again involving a pair of jets supported by a KC-135R forward-deployed from the 459th Air Refueling Wing at Andrews AFB, Maryland. Lt Gen Richard Clark, 3rd Air Force commander, said during a press event after the arrival: 'We routinely train through joint and combined initiatives like Operation 'Atlantic Resolve' and in flying exercises like 'Thracian Eagle', 'Thracian Summer' and 'Thracian Star'. Our commitment to Bulgaria is but an example of our unwavering support to all allied nations. We are grateful to our Bulgarian friends for

their support in making today possible. Your co-operation helps prepare the F-35 for its invaluable contribution to our alliance. We look forward to many more years of our shared commitment and partnership.'

Maj Gen Tsanko Stoykov, Bulgarian Air Force commander, added: 'Our efforts have been appreciated and we are trusted as a reliable ally and it immensely contributes to the development of the bilateral relations between our two counties and our two air forces.'

Lessons learned
Following their arrival in the UK, more extensive missions followed local familiarization alongside the F-15Cs. A

news release said: 'Pilots and maintainers are generating roughly 10 sorties a day, training alongside F-15Cs and F-15Es from the 48th FW, as well as the Royal Air Force and other NATO allies'. The Kadena deployment appears to be following a similar path. Lt Col Jason Zumwalt, who was at the time the commander of the 493rd FS at Lakenheath that was hosting the F-35s, said: 'We've had the opportunity to go out with a building block approach and fly one Eagle with one F-35 fighting each other. Then we built on that and got into the bigger exercises, culminating in today where we had four F-15Cs, four F-15Es and four F-35s plus some RAF Typhoons all working together to accomplish a single mission against a very robust enemy threat. There was simulated air-to-ground going on with some F-15Es striking a target. The F-15Cs led out with the F-35s in an integrated air operation to sweep the airspace of the enemy aircraft and then get the strikers into the simulated targets to drop their bombs, and then escort everybody back out.'

'The sensor fusion capability of the F-35A gives [our F-15s] unprecedented situational awareness which is invaluable when you're fighting against a high-end threat', said Lt Col Scott Taylor, an F-15C pilot with the 'Grim Reapers'. 'The key is it allows us to make quicker, more accurate decisions on targets. We fight best when we fight together. We've had a lot of synergy in our training. When we come back and talk after missions, we can have that face-to-face interaction and review our

This image: **SSgt Frank Anderson, F-35A Crew Chief, greets pilot Capt Tyler McBride.** USAF/Michael McCool

Below: **Led by a 493rd FS F-15C, a 494th FS Strike Eagle and two 34th FS F-35As form up near Lakenheath.** Jamie Hunter

tactics. That's just going to improve the way we fight with the F-35A and has made this an outstanding deployment', Taylor concluded.

'For me, it's my first time dogfighting against an F-15', commented Maj Luke Harris, another F-35A pilot with the 'Rams'. 'Dogfighting is a test of pilot skill, but it's also constrained by the aircraft's capabilities and I've been really impressed by the flight control and maneuverability of the F-35'. He added that the attributes of the F-35 are meant to help avoid an adversary getting to the visual merge and a turning fight. 'All the guys we've flown with have said that having the F-35 in the fight has been an eye-opening experience and they're glad that these capabilities are on their side.'

Summing up the deployment, Lt Col Zumwalt said: 'It's been a great opportunity to exercise fourth- and fifth-generation integration and to give my pilots exposure to what it's like flying with and against the F-35s, plus give their pilots exposure to integrated tactics with the F-15C. One of the lessons I take away every time we integrate fourth- and fifth-gen' assets is that both are very good on their own, but when we get together both of us work much better. Our combined efforts are far superior to what either could do alone. But that takes practice because it's outside the normal everyday habit pattern. So these opportunities to work together really enhance our ability to operate in that pattern in the future.' =★=

Below :
F-35A serial 13-5081 awaits its pilot for a large-force exercise on April 28.
Jamie Hunter

Right: **F-15C 'Wardog 1' breaks into the circuit at Lakenheath as the 'Hill-Lakenheath' team returns to base.**
Jamie Hunter

An in-depth look at the units, bases and aircraft that constitute US Air Force air power in 2018.

report: **Tom Kaminski**

AIR POWER REVIEW

THE US AIR Force and US Army aviation share a common history that can be traced to the creation of the Aeronautical Division, US Army Signal Corps, in 1907. The USAF's history as an independent service began on September 18, 1947 when the Army Air Forces were separated from the US Army. Its establishment was part of a major restructuring of US military forces that was authorized by the National Security Act of 1947.

The service has now been conducting combat operations for more than 26 years. Its aircraft and personnel continue to operate in support of overseas contingency operations (OCO) in Afghanistan, Iraq and Syria and as part of Combined Joint Task Force-Horn of Africa. Recent operations have also been

conducted in Libya, Yemen, Somalia and other locations on the African continent. More than 100,000 airmen are forward-deployed at overseas locations and in support of contingencies. Additionally, in excess of 200,000 directly support combatant commander requirements from their home stations, including more than 30,000 airmen who stand alert '24/7' in support of two legs of the nation's nuclear triad.

The Air Force remains actively engaged in operations against so-called Islamic State (IS) in Iraq and Syria as part of Operation 'Inherent Resolve' (OIR), and continues to provide training and operational support to the Afghan National Defense and Security Forces (ANDSF) as part of Operation 'Freedom's Sentinel' (OFS) and the NATO-led Operation 'Resolute Support' (ORS). Since the campaign against IS began in

2014 the service has typically conducted more than 70 sorties daily and has participated in 70 per cent of the 26,000-plus coalition air strikes in Iraq and Syria.

Released in May 2017, the Department of Defense's $639.1-billion budget request for Fiscal Year 2018 includes $64.6 billion for OCO. The USAF's portion of the request totaled $183 billion. The request provided for a total force of 501,500 personnel and increased the active force by 4,100 and the reserve component by 1,700.

It requested funding for 1,153,309 flying hours and support for a total aircraft inventory (TAI) of 5,416 aircraft, comprising 4,015 in the active component as well as 1,073 in the Air National Guard (ANG) and 328 in Air Force Reserve Command (AFRC). It further provides funding for the

Above: **An F-15E Strike Eagle at low level — an environment that is still regarded as being valuable in high-threat situations.**
Neil Bates

- Air, space and cyberspace superiority
- Intelligence, surveillance and reconnaissance
- Rapid global mobility
- Global strike
- Command and control

The US Air Force's active component (AC) and two reserve components (RC) that include Air Force Reserve Command (AFRC) and the Air National Guard (ANG) comprise the Total Force (TF). The full-time AC comprises approximately 64 per cent of the Total Force, while AFRC and the ANG are responsible for the remainder.

Air Combat Command (ACC) — More than 80,000 active-duty and 11,000 civilian personnel, and over 49,000 members of the ANG and AFRC, are assigned to ACC, which is headquartered at Joint Base Langley-Eustis, Virginia. The command is the primary provider of air combat forces to warfighting commanders. ACC is responsible for five Numbered Air Forces (NAF) that include one staffed by the Air National Guard and another assigned to Air Force Reserve Command. In excess of 1,300 aircraft are assigned to the command, which was created on June 1, 1992, when assets from Strategic Air Command and Tactical Air Command were consolidated.

Air Education and Training Command (AETC) — Headquartered at Joint Base San Antonio-Randolph, Texas, AETC's history can be traced to the formation of the Army Air Corps Flying Training Command, which was established and activated in January 1942. The command is responsible for two NAFs and approximately 1,300 aircraft. More than 29,000 active-duty, 6,000 ANG and AFRC personnel, and 15,000 civilians and 11,000 contractor personnel are assigned to AETC.

Air Force Global Strike Command (AFGSC) — Headquartered at Barksdale AFB, Louisiana, AFGSC is responsible for the nation's intercontinental ballistic missile wings and the operational fleet of B-1B, B-2A and B-52H strategic bombers and E-4B command and control aircraft. Activated on August 7, 2009, its assets are assigned to two NAFs. The command assumed responsibility for the E-4B fleet from ACC in October 2016.

Air Force Materiel Command (AFMC) — Tasked with conducting research, development, test and evaluation, AFMC also provides acquisition management services and logistics support for the Air Force's weapon systems. The command, which was created on July 1, 1992, is headquartered at Wright-Patterson AFB, Ohio. AFMC is responsible for the Air Force Test Center (AFTC) at Edwards AFB, California, the Air Force Life Cycle Management Center (AFLCMC) at Wright-Patterson, the Air Force Sustainment Center (AFSC) at Tinker AFB, Oklahoma and the Air Force Nuclear Weapons Center (AFNWC) at Kirtland AFB, New Mexico. The command's history can be traced to 1917 when the US Army Signal Corps Equipment Division established a headquarters for its newly created Airplane Engineering Department at McCook Field, Dayton, Ohio.

Air Force Reserve Command (AFRC) — The Air Force Reserve was originally established on April 14, 1948. Redesignated as Air Force Reserve Command, it became the USAF's ninth MAJCOM on February 17, 1997. Headquartered at Robins AFB, Georgia, it has more than 30 flying wings. Its associate units are stationed alongside AC units and share responsibility for their aircraft. The command's wings, independent groups and support units are integrated into each of the MAJCOMs. Its three NAFs are aligned with specific mission sets comprising strategic reach, power and vigilance and tactical reach/combat support.

procurement of 85 new manned and unmanned aircraft comprising 46 F-35As, 15 KC-46As, two HC-130Js, five MC-130Js, one EC-X (EC-130H replacement), 16 MQ-9As and six aircraft for the Civil Air Patrol at a cost of $15.3 billion.

Organization

Headquartered at the Pentagon in Arlington, Virginia, the Department of the Air Force is led by the chief of staff of the Air Force. The four-star general is responsible for the organization, training and equipping of active-duty, Air National Guard, Air Force Reserve Command and civilian personnel serving both in the continental United States (CONUS) and overseas. The service is comprised of 10 major commands (MAJCOM) including nine that operate the Air Force's fleet of combat, combat and training aircraft. Each MAJCOM is led by a four-star general or a three-star lieutenant general and is responsible for aircraft and personnel that are tasked in support of one of the service's five interdependent and integrated core missions:

Right: **Block 40/42/50/52 F-16s are set to receive the Northrop Grumman Scalable Agile Beam Radar, which is currently in flight-test at Edwards AFB, California.** Jamie Hunter

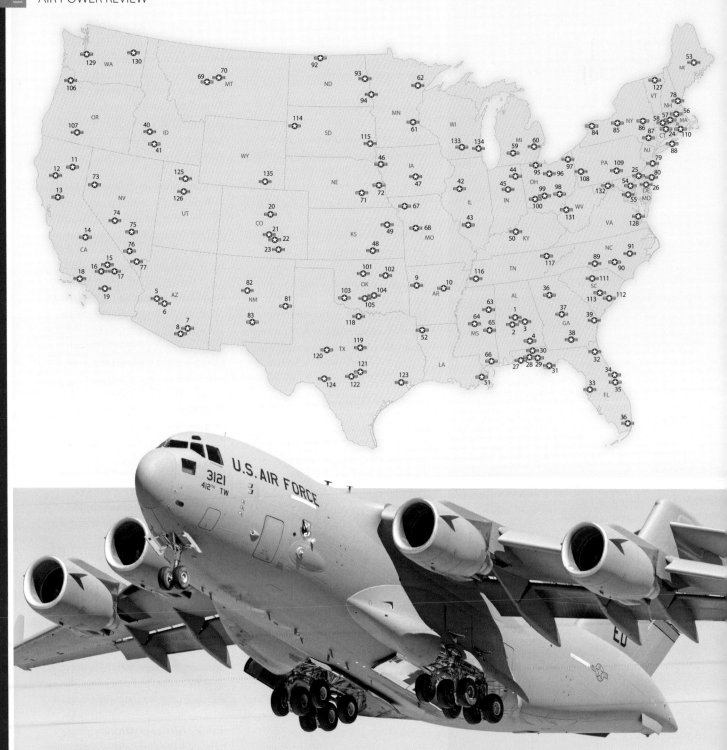

Air Force Space Command (AFSPC)
— Headquartered at Peterson AFB,
Colorado, AFSPC provides space and
cyberspace capabilities. Although more
than 35,000 personnel are assigned to
the command, which was established
on September 1, 1982, it is not currently
responsible for any aircraft. The USAF is,
however, considering merging AFSPC's
24th Air Force/Air Forces Cyber and
ACC's 25th Air Force to consolidate its
cyber and intelligence, surveillance and
reconnaissance assets under a single
command. The 25th AF is responsible
for ACC's fleet of U-2, RQ-4, RC-135 and
EC-130H aircraft.

**Air Force Special Operations
Command (AFSOC)** — Established on
May 22, 1990, AFSOC is the Air Force
component of US Special Operations
Command. More than 19,500 personnel
and around 130 aircraft are currently
assigned to the command, which
is headquartered at Hurlburt Field,
Florida. AFSOC is responsible for five
active-duty special operations wings
and one active-duty special operations
group. Additionally, reserve component
organizations gained by the command
include two special operations
wings assigned to the ANG and one
within AFRC.

Air Mobility Command (AMC) —
Established when assets from Strategic
Air Command and Military Airlift
Command were consolidated on June 1,
1992, AMC is responsible for more than
1,000 airlift aircraft operated by AC, ANG
and AFRC wings, groups and squadrons
under its control. The command is the
air component of US Transportation
Command (USTRANSCOM) and is
headquartered at Scott AFB, Illinois.
AMC is responsible for a single NAF
and in excess of 103,000 personnel.
Headquarters Air Mobility Command
was consolidated with Headquarters
Military Airlift Command (MAC) on

Above:
**The Air Mobility
Command fleet
is dominated
by the C-17A
Globemaster
III, which is the
strategic airlift
workhorse
alongside the
C-5 Galaxy.**
Jamie Hunter

CONTINENTAL US USAF BASE GUIDE

Alabama (AL)
1. Birmingham-Shuttlesworth International Airport
2. Maxwell-Gunter AFB
3. Montgomery Regional Airport-Dannelly Field
4. Lowe AHP, Fort Rucker

Arizona (AZ)
5. Luke AFB
6. Phoenix Sky Harbor International Airport
7. Davis-Monthan AFB
8. Tucson International Airport

Arkansas (AR)
9. Fort Smith Regional Airport/Ebbing ANGB
10. Little Rock AFB

California (CA)
11. Beale AFB
12. Travis AFB
13. Moffett Federal Airport ANGS
14. Fresno-Yosemite International Airport/ANGB
15. Edwards AFB
16. Palmdale/USAF Plant 42
17. Grey Butte FTOF, Palmdale
18. Point Mugu-Channel Islands ANGS
19. March ARB

Colorado (CO)
20. Buckley AFB, Aurora
21. USAFA Airfield, Colorado Springs
22. Peterson AFB
23. Pueblo Memorial Airport

Connecticut (CT)
24 . Bradley IAP/ANGB, Windsor Locks

Delaware (DE)
25. New Castle County Airport
26. Dover AFB

Florida (FL)
27. NAS Pensacola
28. Hurlburt Field
29. Eglin AFB
30. Duke Field
31. Tyndall AFB
32. Jacksonville International Airport
33. MacDill AFB
34. Patrick AFB
35. Melbourne International Airport
36. Homestead ARB

Georgia (GA)
36. Dobbins ARB
37. Robins AFB
38. Moody AFB
39. Savannah Hilton Head IAP

Idaho (ID)
40. Boise Airport-Gowen Field
41. Mountain Home AFB

Illinois (IL)
42. General Downing-Peoria IAP
43. Scott AFB

Indiana (IN)
44. Fort Wayne International Airport
45. Grissom ARB

Iowa (IA)
46. Des Moines International Airport
47. Sioux Gateway/Col Bud Day Field

Kansas (KS)
48. McConnell AFB
49. Forbes Field Airport, Topeka

Kentucky (KY)
50. Louisville IAP-Standiford Field

Louisiana (LA)
51. NAS JRB New Orleans
52. Barksdale AFB

Maine (ME)
53. Bangor International Airport

Maryland (MD)
54. Martin State AP/Warfield ANGB, Baltimore
55. JB Andrews-NAF Washington

Massachusetts (MA)
56. Hanscom AFB
57. Westover ARB
58. Westfield Barnes Airport/ANGB

Michigan (MI)
59. W. K. Kellogg Airport/ANGB, Battle Creek
60. Selfridge ANGB, Mount Clemens

Minnesota (MN)
61. Duluth International Airport/ANGB
62. Minneapolis St Paul IAP/ARS

Mississippi (MS)
63. Columbus AFB
64. Jackson IAP-Allen C. Thompson Field
65. Meridian Regional Airport-Key Field
66. Keesler AFB

Missouri (MO)
67. Rosecrans Municipal Airport, St Joseph
68. Whiteman AFB

Montana (MT)
69. Malmstrom AFB
70. Great Falls International Airport

Nebraska (NE)
71. Lincoln Municipal Airport/ANGB
72. Offutt AFB

Nevada (NV)
73. Reno Tahoe IAP/May ANGB
74. Tonopah Test Range
75. Groom Lake
76. Creech AFB
77. Nellis AFB

New Hampshire (NH)
78. Pease ANGB, Portsmouth IAP

New Jersey (NJ)
79. JB McGuire-Dix-Lakehurst
80. Atlantic City International Airport/ANGB

New Mexico (NM)
81. Cannon AFB
82. Kirtland AFB
83. Holloman AFB

New York (NY)
84. Niagara Falls International Airport/JARS
85. Syracuse Hancock International Airport
86. Schenectady/Stratton ANGS, Scotia
87. Stewart International Airport/ANGB
88. Francis S. Gabreski Airport/ANGB, Westhampton Beach

North Carolina (NC)
89. Charlotte Douglas International Airport
90. Pope AAF, Fort Bragg
91. Seymour Johnson AFB

North Dakota (ND)
92. Minot AFB
93. Grand Forks AFB
94. Hector International Airport, Fargo

Ohio (OH)
95. Toledo Express Airport, Swanton
96. Mansfield Lahm Airport
97. Youngstown Warren Airport/JARS
98. Rickenbacker IAP/ANGB
99. Springfield-Beckley Municipal Airport
100. Wright-Patterson AFB

Oklahoma (OK)
101. Vance AFB
102. Tulsa International Airport
103. Altus AFB
104. Tinker AFB
105. Will Rogers Airport, Oklahoma City

Oregon (OR)
106. Portland International Airport/ANGB
107. Klamath Falls Airport-Kingsley Field

Pennsylvania (PA)
108. Pittsburgh International Airport/JARS
109. Harrisburg International Airport

Rhode Island (RI)
110. Quonset State/Holland ANGB

South Carolina (SC)
111. Shaw AFB
112. JB Charleston
113. McEntire JNGS

South Dakota (SD)
114. Ellsworth AFB
115. Sioux Falls Airport-Joe Foss Field

Tennessee (TN)
116. Memphis International Airport
117. McGhee Tyson/ANGB, Knoxville

Texas (TX)
118. Sheppard AFB
119. NAS JRB Fort Worth/Carswell Field
120. Dyess AFB
121. JB San Antonio-Randolph
122. JB San Antonio-Kelly, Lackland AFB
123. Ellington Field JRB
124. Laughlin AFB

Utah (UT)
125. Hill AFB
126. Wright ANGB/Salt Lake City IAP

Vermont (VT)
127. Burlington International Airport

Virginia (VA)
128. JB Langley-Eustis

Washington (WA)
129. JB Lewis-McChord
130. Fairchild AFB

West Virginia (WV)
131. Yeager Airport, Charleston
132. Shepherd ANGS, Martinsburg

Wisconsin (WI)
133. Dane County-Truax Field, Madison
134. Gen Mitchell IAP/ARS, Milwaukee

Wyoming (WY)
135. Cheyenne Municipal Airport

Below: **The Raptor maintains a useful ground attack role with the GBU-39 Small Diameter Bomb (SDB) and the GBU-32 Joint Direct Attack Munition.** USAF/SSgt Carlin O. Leslie

October 1, 2016. That move made AMC the oldest major command in the Air Force. MAC's own history can be traced back to Air Transport Command, which was created in July 1942.

Pacific Air Forces (PACAF) — Serving as the air component of US Pacific Command, PACAF is headquartered at Joint Base Pearl Harbor-Hickam, Hawaii. Its history goes back to the activation of Far East Air Forces at Brisbane, Queensland, Australia, on August 3, 1944. Three NAFs and around 46,000 personnel are assigned to the command. Its aircraft are based in Hawaii, Alaska, Guam, Japan and the Republic of Korea. PACAF is also responsible for gained ANG and AFRC units in Alaska, Hawaii and Guam.

US Air Forces Europe — Air Forces Africa (USAFE — AFAFRICA) — Headquartered at Ramstein Air Base, Germany, USAFE-AFAFRICA is responsible for a single NAF. More than 35,000 personnel and 200 aircraft are assigned. Since April 20, 2012 the command has been tasked as the air component for both US European Command and US Africa Command. Its current name was assigned when 17th Air Force, which previously served as the air component for US Africa Command (AFRICOM), was inactivated. As part of that move the latter's mission responsibility was transferred to USAFE. The command originated as the 8th Air Force in 1942 and became USAFE in August 1945.

Air National Guard (ANG) — Administered by the National Guard Bureau, the ANG is tasked with both State and Federal missions. It is a joint bureau of the departments of the Army and Air Force and is headquartered at the Pentagon in Arlington, Virginia. The ANG was established as a separate reserve component of the USAF on September 18, 1947, as part of the National Security Act of 1947. The ANG is responsible for units assigned to all 50 states, the District of Columbia and the US Territories of Puerto Rico, the Virgin Islands and Guam. Its flying units are responsible for over 1,050 fixed-wing, rotary-wing and remotely piloted aircraft, and nearly 106,000 personnel are assigned.

AIRCRAFT AND SQUADRONS OF THE US AIR FORCE

An A-10C of the 354th Expeditionary Fighter Squadron in Operation 'Inherent Resolve'. USAF/SSgt Michael Battles

A-10C Thunderbolt II

Beginning in 1976 the USAF accepted the first of 713 A-10As from Fairchild Republic. Deliveries were completed in 1984. After several attempts to retire the type the USAF is now planning to retain the bulk of these close air support aircraft through 2021 or beyond. In fact, in June the air force's chief acquisition officer stated that it was committed to maintaining a minimum of six combat-ready A-10 squadrons through 2030.

Known affectionately as the 'Warthog', the A-10 first saw combat during Operation 'Desert Storm' in January 1991. It subsequently carried out missions over Bosnia, Afghanistan and most recently Syria. After entering service the aircraft received minor upgrades, but between January 2005 and July 2011 around 350 A-10As were upgraded to A-10C configuration under the Precision Engagement

(PE) program. It integrated a MIL-STD-1760 databus, and AN/AAQ-28 Litening and AN/AAQ-33 Sniper targeting pods with a digital stores management system (DSMS) that provided a central interface control unit (CICU), two multi-function color displays (MFCDs) and a new armament/head-up display control panel.

The Maryland Air National Guard's 104th Fighter Squadron achieved initial operational capability (IOC) with the A-10C in August 2007. Additionally, in 2013 the 74th Fighter Squadron fielded a helmet-mounted integrated targeting (HMIT) system and the Gentex Scorpion helmet-mounted cueing system (HMCS), which provides day/night color displays. This is now widespread on the fleet.

The latest Mode 5 identification friend or foe (IFF) capability and Lightweight Airborne Recovery System (LARS) improvements were added in 2015 when operational

Squadron	Location	Aircraft	Wing/Group	Command	Tail code
AATC	Davis-Monthan AFB, Arizona	A-10C	57th Wing/USAFWS	ACC	DP
358th FS (see note 1)	Whiteman AFB, Missouri	A-10C	20th FW/495th FG	ACC	KC
25th FS	Osan AB, Republic of Korea	A-10C	51st FW/OG	PACAF	OS
40th FLTS	Eglin AFB, Florida	A-10C	96th TW/OG	AFMC	ET
66th WPS	Nellis AFB, Nevada	A-10C	57th Wing/USAFWS	ACC	WA
75th FS	Moody AFB, Georgia	A-10C	23rd Wing/23rd FG	ACC	FT
74th FS	Moody AFB, Georgia	A-10C	23rd Wing/23rd FG	ACC	FT
354th FS	Davis-Monthan AFB, Arizona	A-10C	355th FW/OG	ACC	DM
357th FS (FTU)	Davis-Monthan AFB, Arizona	A-10C	355th FW/OG	ACC	DM
422nd TES	Nellis AFB, Nevada	A-10C	53rd Wing/53rd TEG	ACC	OT
Air National Guard units					
104th FS	Martin State Airport/Warfield ANGB, Baltimore, Maryland	A-10C	175th Wing/OG	ACC	MD
107th FS	Selfridge ANGB, Mount Clemens, Michigan	A-10C	127th Wing/OG	ACC	MI
163rd FS	Fort Wayne International Airport, Indiana	A-10C	122nd FW/OG	ACC	IN
190th FS	Boise Airport-Gowen Field, Idaho	A-10C	124th FW/OG	ACC	ID
Air Force Reserve Command units					
47th FS (FTU)	Davis-Monthan AFB, Arizona	A-10C	944th FW/924th FG	ACC	DP
76th FS (see note 2)	Moody AFB, Georgia	A-10C	442nd FW/476th FG	ACC	FT
303rd FS	Whiteman AFB, Missouri	A-10C	442nd FW/OG	ACC	KC
706th FS (see note 2)	Nellis AFB, Nevada	A-10C	926th Wing/OG	ACC	WA

1 Active associate squadron utilizes aircraft assigned to AFRC's 442nd Fighter Wing.
2 Classic associate squadron utilizes aircraft assigned to host wing.

flight program (OFP) suite 8 was released.

There are currently 281 A-10Cs in service with 18 active USAF, ANG and AFRC units. A total of 49 A-10Cs and 46 unmodified A-10As remain in storage with the 309th AMARG at Davis-Monthan AFB, Arizona. Although around 170 of the aircraft

received new wings that were produced by Boeing as part of its previous attempts to retire the A-10, the USAF cut the program short of its goal. As a result, more than 100 aircraft still need new wings. Funding to restart the modification was requested in the USAF's Fiscal 2018 budget.

B-2A Spirit

First flown in July 1989, the B-2A entered service in December 1993 and saw its maiden combat over Kosovo in March 1999. The bombers have flown more than 3,000 hours in combat, most recently in attacks against Islamic State targets in Libya.

Originally known as the Advanced Technology Bomber (ATB), development of the low-observable aircraft began in November 1981 when Northrop received a $7.3-billion contract. The initial B-2A

was publicly unveiled in Palmdale, California in November 1988.

The aircraft were first delivered in Block 10 configuration with a limited combat capability that included 2,000lb (907kg) Mk84 conventional bombs or gravity nuclear weapons. The Block 20-configured aircraft that followed featured an interim capability to deliver the GPS-Aided Munition (GAM). The final Block 30 configuration provided full capability, which included additional radar modes, enhanced terrain-

following capability and additional weapons capabilities via the Joint Direct Attack Munition (JDAM) and the Joint Stand-Off Weapon (JSOW). Since delivery, the entire fleet has received incremental upgrades that added further capabilities. Under those efforts, the bombers have received new communications capabilities, upgraded radar and additional weapons that include the 30,000lb (13,608kg) 'bunker-busting' GBU-57 Massive Ordnance Penetrator (MOP).

Upgrades will add a new satellite communications system, computers and even more weapons capabilities. The largest effort will update the B-2A's defensive management system, while the Spirit will be the first aircraft to use the precision-guided B61-12 (LEP) nuclear bomb.

The original plan for a fleet of 132 B-2As was reduced dramatically and only 21 were delivered. Currently, 20 are flown by eight test, training and operational squadrons that include a single ANG associate squadron.

B-1B Lancer

The B-1B originally reached initial operational capability in October 1986 and the last of 100 examples was delivered during May 1988. Currently, 62 aircraft are operated by eight active-duty squadrons and a single AFRC associate squadron. Additionally, 18 B-1Bs are stored at Davis-Monthan AFB, Arizona.

Although it was designed to penetrate Soviet defenses and deliver nuclear weapons, since 1997 the B-1B has been limited to delivering conventional weapons. The versatile, long-range, multi-mission bomber carries the largest payload of both guided and unguided conventional weapons in the USAF inventory. The Lancer was the first aircraft to field the Lockheed Martin AGM-158B Joint Air-to-Surface Stand-off Missile-Extended Range (JASSM-ER) and will be the initial platform for the AGM-158C Long-Range Anti-Ship Missile (LRASM), which will enter service in 2018. The B-1B first tested the LRASM against a maritime target on the Point Mugu Sea Range in August 2017.

Since entering service in June 1985, the bombers have received several upgrades including the Conventional Mission Upgrade Program (CMUP) that enabled it to deliver precision-guided weapons. Subsequent programs provided the Lancer with upgrades to its defensive countermeasures system and the ability to carry a Sniper targeting pod. The fleet is currently being upgraded under the integrated battle station (IBS) and Sustainment Block 16 (SB 16)

A B-1B assigned to the 9th Expeditionary Bomb Squadron, deployed from Dyess AFB, Texas, takes off from Andersen AFB, Guam, on June 22, 2017. USAF/TSgt Richard P. Ebensberger

project. The $1-billion program is the largest modification yet developed for the B-1B, and is intended to improve situational awareness and battlefield communication, reduce crew workload and support evolving network-centric warfare. It provides the bomber with time-critical targeting and precision engagement capabilities. The modifications will allow the Lancer to remain viable until it is replaced by the B-21A.

According to the Air Force, testing has determined that the B-1B can operate through 2040 without requiring an expensive life extension. The Lancer was originally designed to fly 9,681 equivalent flight hours (EFH), but its service life is currently projected to reach 19,900 hours.

Dyess AFB received the first operational B-1B to receive the IBS modifications in January 2014. Initial operational capability was achieved following delivery of the 15th Lancer to the base in December 2015.

Squadron	Location	Aircraft	Wing/Group	Command	Tail code
9th BS	Dyess AFB, Texas	B-1B	7th BW/OG	AFGSC	DY
28th BS (FTU)	Dyess AFB, Texas	B-1B	7th BW/OG	AFGSC	DY
31st TES (see note 1)	Edwards AFB, California	B-1B	53rd Wing/53rd TEG	ACC	ED
34th BS	Ellsworth AFB, South Dakota	B-1B	28th BW/OG	AFGSC	EL
37th BS	Ellsworth AFB, South Dakota	B-1B	28th BW/OG	AFGSC	EL
77th WPS	Dyess AFB, Texas	B-1B	57th Wing/USAFWS	ACC	WA
337th TES (see note 2)	Dyess AFB, Texas	B-1B	53rd Wing/53rd TEG	ACC	DY
419th FLTS	Edwards AFB, California	B-1B	412th TW/OG	AFMC	ED
Air Force Reserve Command units					
345th BS (see note 3)	Dyess AFB, Texas	B-1B	307th BW/489th BG	AFRC	DY

1	Squadron utilizes aircraft assigned to 419th FLTS.
2	Squadron utilizes aircraft assigned to 28th BW.
3	Classic associate squadron utilizes aircraft assigned to the 7th BW.

Around 10 B-1Bs are receiving the upgrades annually during programmed depot maintenance with the Oklahoma City Air Logistics Complex at Tinker AFB, Oklahoma. As of October 2017, 32 B-1Bs had been modernized, and the program will be completed by 2019.

The B-1B is also being equipped with the Rockwell Collins Multi-functional Information Distribution System-Joint Tactical Radio System (MIDS-JTRS) terminal, which provides the aircraft with improved

communications and networking. The type will be further upgraded with Mode 5 identification friend or foe (IFF) and automatic dependent surveillance-broadcast (ADS-B Out), allowing it to meet the Federal Aviation Administration (FAA)'s NextGen air traffic control mandates.

The USAF intends to replace the Lancer's AN/APQ-164 radar with a new active electronically scanned array (AESA) system based on the AN/APG-83, which Northrop Grumman developed for the F-16 Fighting Falcon.

Squadron	Location	Aircraft	Wing/Group	Command	Tail code
13th BS	Whiteman AFB, Missouri	B-2A	509th BW/OG	AFGSC	WM
31st TES (see note 1)	Edwards AFB, California	B-2A	53rd Wing/53rd TEG	ACC	ED
72nd TES (see note 1)	Whiteman AFB, Missouri	B-2A	53rd Wing/53rd TEG	ACC	WM
325th WPS (see note 1)	Whiteman AFB, Missouri	B-2A	53rd Wing/53rd TEG	ACC	DY
393rd BS	Whiteman AFB, Missouri	B-2A	509th BW/OG	AFGSC	WM
394th CTS (FTU) (see note 2)	Whiteman AFB, Missouri	B-2A	509th BW/OG	AFGSC	WM
419th FLTS	Edwards AFB, California	B-2A	412th TW/OG	AFMC	ED
Air National Guard units					
110th BS (see note 3)	Whiteman AFB, Missouri	B-2A	131st BW/OG	AFGSC	WM

1	Squadron utilizes aircraft assigned to host wing.
2	394th CTS utilizes 325th/393rd BS B-2As for training.
3	Classic associate squadron utilizes aircraft assigned to the 509th BW.

A B-2A Spirit of the 509th Bomb Wing at Whiteman AFB. USAF/SSgt Colton Flliott

B-21A Raider

The USAF announced that Northrop Grumman would build a new Long-Range Strike Bomber (LRS-B) on October 27, 2015. The aircraft, which was subsequently assigned the designation B-21A Raider, will be an integral component in the service's future long-range strike family of systems. Although little has been revealed about the aircraft, its configuration is similar to the B-2A and the bomber is expected to employ mature technologies but will feature stealth capabilities, carry a large payload and conduct conventional and nuclear deterrent missions.

The USAF and Northrop Grumman completed a preliminary design review in early 2017. Under current plans the bomber will achieve initial operational capability (IOC) in the mid-2020s. The B-21A will initially be limited to carrying conventional stand-off and direct attack weapons but will be certified to carry nuclear weapons within two years of the initial conventional IOC declaration.

The acquisition of the B-21A remains one of the USAF's top three acquisition programs and procurement of 80-100 or more aircraft is planned. The first five production lots will comprise a total of 21 aircraft that will be purchased under a fixed price incentive contract. The bombers are expected to have an average procurement cost of $564 million in 2016 dollars.

An artist's rendition of the B-21A Raider. USAF

B-52H Stratofortress

Developed as a high-altitude, long range strategic bomber, the Boeing B-52 first flew in prototype form during 1954 and entered operational USAF service in 1955. When the last of 102 B-52Hs was accepted in October 1962, Boeing had delivered 744 examples in eight major versions. The bomber is the longest-serving combat aircraft in US history. Today only the B-52H remains in the inventory and 75 examples of the type are in service. The total includes 18 that are assigned to AFRC and two that support ongoing testing.

Since the first B-52H was delivered in May 1961, the aircraft has received many upgrades that allowed it to be adapted for new missions that were not foreseen when it was designed.

The USAF intends to operate the Stratofortress until the 2040s and the fleet is receiving upgrades that will allow the bomber to remain viable. Known as the Combat Network Communications Technology (CONECT), the update greatly enhances the aircraft's combat capabilities in the digital battlespace. It provides new multi-functional color displays (MFCDs), computer architecture, multiple datalinks and enhanced voice communications capabilities. The CONECT modifications are carried out during programmed depot maintenance (PDM) at the Oklahoma City Air Logistics Complex (OC-ALC) at Tinker AFB, Oklahoma. Modifications to an initial B-52H were completed at Tinker in mid-2014 and the aircraft was first deployed to combat in September 2016.

Providing the capability to conduct network-centric operations (NCO), CONECT allows B-52H crews to receive and send real-time digital information including intelligence, mapping and targeting information, and to communicate with other platforms via satellite. The integrated suite enables mission re-tasking and weapons re-targeting for the AGM-86C/D Conventional Air-Launched Cruise Missile (CALCM) and AGM-158 Joint Air-to-Surface Stand-off Missile/JASSM-Extended Range (JASSM/JASSM-ER) weapons.

The type's weapons payload of more than 70,000lb (31,751kg) allows it to carry the most diverse range of nuclear and conventional weapons of any combat aircraft in the inventory. To meet the requirements of the New START nuclear weapons treaty, the ability to deliver nuclear weapons is being removed from 30 operational bombers and 13 that are stored with the 309th Aerospace Maintenance and Regeneration Group at Davis-Monthan AFB, Arizona.

Although the USAF has not formally established a program of record, the service is considering replacing the B-52H's Pratt & Whitney TF33 turbofan engines. The cost to re-engine the aircraft has been estimated at $5-7 billion.

B-52Hs are flown by nine USAF operational and test squadrons and a single AFRC unit, which is tasked as the Formal Training Unit (FTU) for the aircraft. An active associate USAF squadron carries out this role alongside the AFRC unit. The fleet of 44 combat-coded bombers is shared by two operational wings comprising the 2nd Bomb Wing at Barksdale AFB, Louisiana and the 5th Bomb Wing at Minot AFB, North Dakota.

Four operational squadrons are each assigned 11 combat-coded aircraft and two airframes that are carried as back-up aircraft inventory (BAI).

Squadron	Location	Aircraft	Wing/Group	Command	Tail code
11th BS (FTU) (see note 1)	Barksdale AFB, Louisiana	B-52H	2nd BW/OG	AFGSC	LA
20th BS	Barksdale AFB, Louisiana	B-52H	2nd BW/OG	AFGSC	LA
23rd BS	Minot AFB, North Dakota	B-52H	5th BW/OG	AFGSC	MT
49th TES	Barksdale AFB, Louisiana	B-52H	53rd Wing/53rd TEG	ACC	OT
69th BS	Minot AFB, North Dakota	B-52H	5th BW/OG	AFGSC	MT
96th BS	Barksdale AFB, Louisiana	B-52H	2nd BW/OG	AFGSC	LA
31st TES (see note 2)	Edwards AFB, California	B-52H	53rd Wing/53rd TEG	ACC	ED
340th WPS (see note 2)	Barksdale AFB, Louisiana	B-52H	53rd Wing/53rd TEG	ACC	LA
419th FLTS	Edwards AFB, California	B-52H	412th TW/OG	AFMC	ED
Air Force Reserve Command units					
93rd BS (FTU)	Barksdale AFB, Louisiana	B-52H	307th BW/OG	AFGSC	BD

1 Active associate squadron utilizes aircraft assigned to AFRC's 93rd BS.
2 Squadron utilizes aircraft assigned to the host wing.

An unmarked B-52H at Al Udeid Air Base, Qatar, in September 2017. USAF/TSgt Amy M. Lovgren

C-5M Galaxy

The first operational C-5A was delivered to the USAF's Military Airlift Command in June 1970 and the last A-model in service with AFRC's 439th Airlift Wing was finally retired on September 7, 2017. As the largest airlifter in the USAF's inventory the Galaxy can carry outsized cargo over intercontinental ranges.

Although the service received 81 C-5As, a shortfall in airlift aircraft resulted in re-starting Galaxy production. That decision led to 50 improved C-5Bs being delivered from January 1986 to March 1989.

Between 2002 and 2012, 27 C-5As, 50 C-5Bs and two C-5Cs were updated with a modern digital cockpit, under the Avionics Modernization Program (AMP). Development of further upgrades under the Reliability Enhancement and Re-engining Program (RERP) began in late 2001. Whereas the original plans called for upgrading more than 120 C-5s under the RERP, ultimately a C-5A, two C-5Cs and 49 C-5Bs will be involved. The C-5A and two C-5Bs served as prototypes.

Carried out by Lockheed Martin at its Marietta, Georgia, facility, the program replaces the Galaxy's General Electric TF39 turbofans with General Electric F138-GE-100 (CF6-80C2) engines that provide 22 per cent more power. In addition to more than 50 improvements to the aircraft's structure and systems, the RERP adds a more powerful auxiliary power unit and installs the Northrop Grumman AN/AAQ-24 Large Aircraft Infra-Red Countermeasures (LAIRCM) system. Changes to airlift fleet requirements resulted in the decision to scale back the program and retire the C-5A fleet. Upgraded C-5Ms are operational with two active-duty USAF squadrons and shared with a pair of AFRC associate squadrons. Two additional AFRC squadrons are transitioning to the C-5M. In September 2017, Lockheed Martin had delivered 46 upgraded C-5Ms while five C-5Bs and one C-5C were undergoing modification. Two C-5Cs were originally created by removing the troop compartments from two C-5As, which allowed them to transport USAF and NASA space program cargo. Once modified under RERP the C-5Cs are known as a C-5M Space Cargo Modified (SCM).

Follow-on upgrades will replace the C-5's core mission computer (CMC) and weather radar to mitigate obsolescence of the existing systems.

Squadron	Location	Aircraft	Wing/Group	Command	Tail code
9th AS	Dover AFB, Delaware	C-5M	436th AW/OG	AMC	
22nd AS	Travis AFB, California	C-5M	60th AMW/OG	AMC	
Air Force Reserve Command units					
312th AS (see note 1)	Travis AFB, California	C-5M	349th AMW/OG	AMC	
68th AS	JB San Antonio-Lackland (Kelly Field), Texas	C-5M	433rd AW/OG	AMC	
326th AS (see note 1)	Dover AFB, Delaware	C-5M	512th AW/OG	AMC	
337th AS	Westover ARB, Massachusetts	C-5M	439th AW/OG	AMC	
356th AS (FTU)	JB San Antonio-Lackland (Kelly Field), Texas	C-5M	433rd AW/OG	AMC	

1   Classic associate squadron utilizes aircraft assigned to host wing.

A communications vehicle is directed on to a C-5M Super Galaxy to be flown to Puerto Rico and assist in disaster relief efforts. USAF/TSgt Kelly Goonan

KC-10A Extender

The McDonnell Douglas DC-10 was selected as the winner of the Advanced Tanker/Cargo Aircraft (ATCA) competition in December 1977. Assigned the military designation KC-10A, the first Extender entered service at March AFB, California, in October 1981. When production ended in November 1988, McDonnell Douglas, which became a part of the Boeing Company in 1997, had delivered 60 KC-10As to the USAF.

The Extender shared 88 per cent systems commonality with the commercial DC-10-30CF airliner. The aircraft is powered by three General Electric CF6-50C2 turbofan engines, which each deliver 52,500lb st (233.5kN) of thrust, and can carry more than 356,000lb (160,200kg) of fuel, nearly doubling the capacity of the smaller KC-135. It features an aerial refueling boom, internal and wing-mounted hose and drogue, aerial refueling operator station, aerial refueling receptacle and satellite communications. The hose and drogue refueling systems allow the KC-10A to refuel a wide variety of US and allied military aircraft during a single mission.

The Extender can combine the tasks of a tanker and cargo platform by refueling aircraft while simultaneously carrying support personnel and equipment on overseas deployments. The KC-10A is in fact capable of transporting up to 75 personnel and nearly 170,000lb (76,560kg) of cargo for around 4,400 miles (7,040km) unrefueled.

The entire KC-10 fleet, which currently includes 59 aircraft, has undergone a communication navigation surveillance/air traffic management (CNS/ATM) upgrade. Installation of the new avionics, which include the Rockwell Collins Flight2 integrated avionics system, made the Extenders compliant with new CNS/ATM mandates for accessing global airspace. The modifications were carried out by Field Aviation at its facility in Oklahoma City, Oklahoma.

Extenders are operated by four USAF and four AFRC associate squadrons at Joint Base McGuire-Dix-Lakehurst, New Jersey and Travis AFB, California.

A KC-10 Extender of the 76th Air Refueling Squadron. USAF/MSgt Mark C. Olsen

Squadron	Location	Aircraft	Wing/Group	Command	Tail code
2nd ARS	JB McGuire-Dix-Lakehurst, New Jersey	KC-10A	305th AMW/OG	AMC	
6th ARS	Travis AFB, California	KC-10A	60th AMW/OG	AMC	
9th ARS	Travis AFB, California	KC-10A	60th AMW/OG	AMC	
32nd ARS	JB McGuire-Dix-Lakehurst, New Jersey	KC-10A	305th AMW/OG	AMC	
Air Force Reserve Command units					
70th ARS (see note 1)	Travis AFB, California	KC-10A	349th AMW/OG	AMC	
76th ARS (see note 1)	JB McGuire-Dix-Lakehurst, New Jersey	KC-10A	514th AMW/OG	AMC	
78th ARS (see note 1)	JB McGuire-Dix-Lakehurst, New Jersey	KC-10A	514th AMW/OG	AMC	
79th ARS (see note 1)	Travis AFB, California	KC-10A	349th AMW/OG	AMC	

1   Classic associate squadron utilizes aircraft assigned to host wing.

Squadron	Location	Aircraft	Wing/Group	Command	Tail code
DIA Air Operations (see note 1)	Wright-Patterson AFB, Ohio	C-12C/D	AFSAC/HQ DIA	AFMC	
DSCA (see note 1)	Wright-Patterson AFB, Ohio	C-12C/D	AFSAC	AFMC	
Det 1, 517th AS	JB Elmendorf-Richardson, Alaska	C-12F	3rd Wing/OG	PACAF	
1st AS	JB Andrews-NAF Washington, Maryland	C-12C	89th AW/OG	AMC	
419th FLTS (see note 2)	Edwards AFB, California	C-12C	412th TW/OG	AFMC	ED
459th AS	Yokota AB, Japan	C-12J	374th AW/OG	PACAF	
586th FLTS	Holloman AFB, New Mexico	C-12J	AEDC/704th TESTG	AFMC	HT
Air National Guard units					
185th SOS	Will Rogers ANGB/World Airport, Oklahoma City, Oklahoma	MC-12W	137th SOW/SOG	AFSOC	

1 DIA/DSCA aircraft operated from numerous worldwide sites.
2 C-12Cs are maintained by NASA Dryden. 419th FLTS is also the FTU for the USAF C-12C/D.

Beechcraft C-12C/D/F/J Huron, MC-12W Liberty

The Beechcraft King Air has been on the USAF inventory since the A200 version was selected to fulfill the CX-X requirement in 1975. Initially acquired as the C-12A, the aircraft received the designation C-12C after being equipped with a more powerful version of the Pratt & Whitney Canada PT6A turboprop. The service later acquired six King Air B200s, under the designation C-12D. Tasked to support US embassies and military attaches worldwide, the bulk of the original aircraft, comprising 16 C-12Cs and six C-12Ds, remain in service.

The USAF later acquired 46 King Air B200Cs and six B1900C airliners for use in the Operational Support Airlift (OSA) role beginning in 1984. During 1996 the bulk of the aircraft, which received the designations C-12F and C-12J were later transferred to the US Army. The USAF retained a handful of the aircraft and its inventory currently includes two C-12Fs and four C-12Js.

As part of Project Liberty, the USAF acquired the first of 42 King Air 350s that were converted into MC-12W intelligence, surveillance and reconnaissance (ISR) aircraft beginning in November 2008. The MC-12W featured a variety of sensors and systems that included electro-optical/infra-red (EO/IR) with a laser pointer. The aircraft had a line-of-sight datalink for remote video terminals (RVT), a limited signals intelligence (SIGINT) collection capability and a narrowband Inmarsat datalink for beyond line-of-sight connectivity. They could transmit full motion video (FMV).

The USAF flew its last missions with the MC-12W in Afghanistan in October 2014 when the US Army's Joint Task Force Thor assumed responsibility for the deployed aircraft. The draw-down of operations in Afghanistan resulted in the USAF's decision to divest the MC-12W fleet. As a result, most of the aircraft were transferred to USSOCOM and eight of them reassigned to the US Army. The USAF, however, retained 13 Liberty aircraft that have been assigned to the Oklahoma Air National Guard's 137th Special Operations Wing. It received its first example in July 2015.

USAF MC-12Ws are assigned to the 185th SOS, Oklahoma ANG. USAF

C-17A Globemaster III

First flown in September 1991, the C-17A entered service when the initial production aircraft was delivered to Charleston AFB, South Carolina, in June 1993. Development of the C-17A began in August 1981 following the selection of McDonnell Douglas as the winner of the C-X competition. The Globemaster III achieved initial operational capability in January 1995 and Boeing, which acquired McDonnell Douglas in 1997, delivered the last of 223 examples to the USAF at Charleston in September 2013.

The C-17A can conduct both inter- and intra-theater missions by delivering troops and cargo to main operating bases or directly to forward bases in the deployment area. Additionally, it can perform tactical airlift and air-drop missions and can operate from smaller, austere airfields. Recent upgrades have installed the Large Infra-Red Countermeasures (LAIRCM) system and new weather radar.

The USAF's current fleet of 222 C-17As is stationed at 14 locations and flown operationally by 11 active-duty, 12 AFRC and six ANG airlift squadrons. The airlifters are also on the strength of two training squadrons, a flight test squadron and a weapons squadron. One ANG and nine of the AFRC squadrons are associate squadrons that operate alongside active-duty units. Likewise, a single active associate squadron operates alongside an ANG unit. The number of C-17As assigned to the ANG and AFRC will increase when the North Carolina Air National Guard's 145th Airlift Wing and the AFRC's 911th Airlift Wing in Pittsburgh, Pennsylvania transition from the C-130H to the C-17A. The aircraft for these units were made available by the inactivation of two active-duty airlift squadrons at Joint Base Lewis-McChord, Washington and Charleston.

A C-17A Globemaster III from Joint Base Charleston taxiing at Travis AFB, on September 11, 2017. USAF/Louis Briscese

C-20H Gulfstream IV

Following the acquisition of 13 Gulfstream IIIs under the designations C-20A, C-20B and C-20C, the USAF purchased two Gulfstream IVs. They were assigned the designation C-20H and initially assigned to the 89th Airlift Wing at Andrews AFB, Maryland. The C-20Cs were retired in late 2013 and the final pair of C-20Bs followed suit in August 2017.

Last operated by the 86th Airlift Wing at Ramstein, Germany, both C-20Hs were retired in September 2017. One went to the US Army; the second was placed on the civil register and transferred to the Air Force Life Cycle Management Center at Hanscom AFB. Three C-20Bs used in the special air mission (SAM) role with the 99th AS at Andrews AFB, Maryland, were retired on August 30, 2017.

Squadron	Location	Aircraft	Wing/Group	Command	Tail code
AFLCMC (See note 1)	Hanscom AFB, Massachusetts	C-20H		AFMC	

1 C-20H operated by Massachusetts Institute of Technology — Lincoln Laboratory.

Squadron	Location	Aircraft	Wing/Group	Command	Tail code
3rd AS	Dover AFB, Delaware	C-17A	436th AW/OG	AMC	
4th AS	JB Lewis-McChord, Washington	C-17A	62nd AW/OG	AMC	
6th AS	JB McGuire-Dix-Lakehurst, New Jersey	C-17A	305th AMW/OG	AMC	
7th AS	JB Lewis-McChord, Washington	C-17A	62nd AW/OG	AMC	
8th AS	JB Lewis-McChord, Washington	C-17A	62nd AW/OG	AMC	
14th AS	JB Charleston, South Carolina	C-17A	437th AW/OG	AMC	
15th AS	JB Charleston, South Carolina	C-17A	437th AW/OG	AMC	
16th AS	JB Charleston, South Carolina	C-17A	437th AW/OG	AMC	
21st AS	Travis AFB, California	C-17A	60th AMW/OG	AMC	
57th WPS (see note 1)	JB Lewis McChord, Washington	C-17A	57th Wing/USAFWS	ACC	
58th AS (FTU)	Altus AFB, Oklahoma	C-17A	97th AMW/OG	AETC	
418th FLTS	Edwards AFB, California	C-17A	412th TW/OG	AFMC	
517th AS (see note 3)	JB Elmendorf-Richardson, Alaska	C-17A	3rd Wing/OG	PACAF	AK
535th AS	JB Pearl Harbor-Hickam, Hawaii	C-17A	15th Wing/OG	PACAF	HH
Air National Guard units					
204th AS (see note 2)	JB Pearl Harbor-Hickam, Hawaii	C-17A	154th Wing/OG	PACAF	HH
249th AS	JB Elmendorf-Richardson, Alaska	C-17A	176th Wing/OG	PACAF	AK
137th AS	Stewart International Airport/ANGB, Newburgh, New York	C-17A	105th AW/OG	AMC	
155th AS	Memphis International Airport, Tennessee	C-17A	164th AW/OG	AMC	
167th AS	Eastern West Virginia Regional Airport/Shepherd ANGS, Martinsburg, West Virginia	C-17A	167th AW/OG	AMC	
183rd AS	Jackson International Airport-Allen C. Thompson Field, Mississippi	C-17A	172nd AW/OG	AMC	
Air Force Reserve Command units					
89th AS	Wright-Patterson AFB, Ohio	C-17A	445th AW/OG	AMC	
97th AS	JB Lewis-McChord, Washington	C-17A	446th AW/OG	AMC	
300th AS (see note 4)	JB Charleston, South Carolina	C-17A	315th AW/OG	AMC	
301st AS (see note 4)	Travis AFB, California	C-17A	349th AMW/OG	AMC	
313th AS (see note 4)	JB Lewis-McChord, Washington	C-17A	446th AW/OG	AMC	
317th AS (see note 4)	JB Charleston, South Carolina	C-17A	315th AW/OG	AMC	
701st AS (see note 4)	JB Charleston, South Carolina	C-17A	315th AW/OG	AMC	
709th AS (see note 4)	Dover AFB, Delaware	C-17A	512th AW/OG	AMC	
728th AS (see note 4)	JB Lewis-McChord, Washington	C-17A	446th AW/OG	AMC	
729th AS	March ARB, California	C-17A	452nd AMW/OG	AMC	
730th AMTS (see note 5)	Altus AFB, Oklahoma	C-17A	507th ARW/OG	AETC	
732nd AS (see note 4)	JB McGuire-Dix-Lakehurst, New Jersey	C-17A	514th AMW/OG	AMC	

1	Squadron utilizes aircraft assigned to host wing.
2	Squadron operates C-17A as an associate to the co-located 535th AS.
3	Squadron operates C-17A as an active associate to the co-located 249th AS.
4	Classic associate squadron utilizes aircraft assigned to host wing.
5	Classic associate squadron supports 97th AMW C-17 training operations.

VC-25A

The USAF operates two modified Boeing 747-200B airliners, under the designation VC-25A, in support of the Presidential airlift mission. The jets were purchased in 1982 and the initial aircraft flew its first mission as 'Air Force One' in September 1990. The aircraft received many modifications that included accommodation for the president and his staff. These include an executive suite that features a stateroom (complete with a dressing room, lavatory and shower), a conference/dining room, medical facility and the president's office. The VC-25s are assigned to the 89th Airlift Wing's Presidential Airlift Group at Andrews AFB, Maryland, and flown by dedicated aircrew from the Presidential Airlift Squadron.

A replacement platform is being developed by Boeing under the USAF's Presidential Aircraft Recapitalization (PAR) program. The new aircraft, based on the 747-800 airliner, was selected by the USAF in January 2015 and recently assigned the designation VC-25B. It is expected to enter service in 2024. Preliminary design work began when Boeing received a $600-million contract in September 2017.

The USAF recently acquired a pair of 747-8 series aircraft that had been ordered by Russian carrier Transaero Airlines in December 2013 but were never delivered to the company, which filed for bankruptcy and ceased operations in October 2015. They had been stored at the Southern California Logistics Airport in Victorville since February 2017.

The aircraft will be outfitted with the many of the same features as the VC-25A including a mission communications system, electrical power upgrades, a medical facility, an executive interior, self-defense system, and autonomous ground operations capabilities. Unlike the current aircraft, however, it will not be equipped for in-flight refueling. Aircraft modifications are expected to begin in 2019.

Squadron	Location	Aircraft	Wing/Group	Command	Tail code
PAS	JB Andrews-NAF Washington, Maryland	VC-25A	89th AW/PAG	AMC	

The USAF operates a pair of VC-25As with the 89th AW. USAF

C-21A Learjet

The USAF operates 22 C-21As in the operational support airlift (OSA) role. Initially leased, the first of 80 C-21As were delivered in April 1984 before the entire fleet was purchased outright at the conclusion of the lease period. Four additional examples were acquired for the Air National Guard in 1986.

Tasked with providing priority cargo and passenger airlift, the operational fleet of USAF Learjets is currently assigned to three units stationed in the CONUS and another located in Germany. The service has disposed of numerous aircraft via General Services Administration (GSA) auctions or transferred them to organizations and schools, but 23 C-21As are retained in storage at Davis-Monthan AFB, Arizona.

Members of the Qatar Emiri Air Force board a C-21A at Al Udeid Air Base, Qatar. USAF/TSgt James Hodgman

Squadron	Location	Aircraft	Wing/Group	Command	Tail code
76th AS	Ramstein AB, Germany	C-21A	86th AW/OG	USAFE	
457th AS	JB Andrews-NAF Washington, Maryland	C-21A	375th AW/OG	AMC	
458th AS (FTU)	Scott AFB, Illinois	C-21A	375th AW/OG	AMC	
Air National Guard units					
200th AS (see note 1)	Peterson AFB, Colorado Springs, Colorado	C-21A	140th Wing	AMC	

1	140th Wing is ACC-gained.

RC-26B Condor

The USAF operates 11 Fairchild Aircraft SA227DC Metroliners. The aircraft have been modified for intelligence, surveillance and reconnaissance (ISR) missions under the designation RC-26B. The Metroliners were originally configured as operational support aircraft but later equipped with semi-permanent modifications comprising sensors, communications equipment and aircraft survivability equipment (ASE). These replaced a removable reconnaissance pod and operator station that allowed the C-26Bs to be tasked with counter-drug (CD) missions. The aircraft have since also taken on additional duties and now operate both in the US and overseas.

The USAF initially procured 11 SA227AC Metroliners for use in the Air National Guard

Squadron	Location	Aircraft	Wing/Group	Command	Tail code
Air National Guard units					
Det 1, 130th AS	Harrison/Marion Regional Airport, West Virginia	RC-26B	130th AW/OG	AMC	
100th FS	Montgomery Regional Airport-Dannelly Field, Alabama	RC-26B	187th FW/OG	ACC	
111th RS	Ellington Field JRB, Houston, Texas	RC-26B	147th RW/OG	ACC	
116th ARS	Fairchild AFB, Washington	RC-26B	141st ARW/OG	AMC	
124th ATKS	Des Moines International Airport, Iowa	RC-26B	132nd Wing/OG	ACC	
148th FS	Tucson International Airport, Arizona	RC-26B	162nd FW/214th ATKG	AETC	
153rd ARS	Meridian Regional Airport-Key Field, Mississippi	RC-26B	186th ARW/OG	AMC	
159th FS	Jacksonville International Airport, Florida	RC-26B	125th FW/OG	ACC	
176th FS	Dane County Regional Airport-Truax Field, Madison, Wisconsin	RC-26B	115th FW/OG	ACC	
188th RQS	Kirtland AFB, New Mexico	RC-26B	150th SOW/OG	AFSOC	
194th FS	Fresno-Yosemite International Airport/ ANGB, California	RC-26B	144th FW/OG	ACC	

Operational Support Transport Aircraft (ANGOSTA) role in 1986, but all of the original examples have been divested. Today the RC-26Bs support combatant command (COCOM) overseas contingency operations (OCO), and provide incident awareness and assessment (IAA) for disaster response, national special security events (NSSE), south-west border operations (SWB), and CD missions. They are assigned to 11 different Air National Guard squadrons.

The 141st Operations Group RC-26B.
USAF/SrA Sean Campbell

C-32A/B

The Boeing 757-200ER-series airliner was selected to replace the USAF's long-serving fleet of VC-137Cs in the Special Air Mission (SAM) role in August 1996. The first of four aircraft entered the inventory under the designation C-32A in June 1998. The extended-range aircraft are normally tasked to carry the vice-president, cabinet members and members of Congress traveling on government business. In addition to carrying up to 45 passengers and a crew of 16 the aircraft is equipped with a communications center, a fully enclosed stateroom, conference and staff facility and general seating with 32 business-class seats. The four C-32As are assigned to the 89th Airlift Wing's 1st Airlift Squadron at Andrews AFB, Maryland, along with three additional 757-200s acquired from commercial sources in 2010. The latter aircraft are not on the Air Force inventory.

The New Jersey Air National Guard operates a pair of 757-200 aircraft under the designation C-32B in support of US Special Operations Command (USSOCOM). Unlike the C-32As, which are powered by two Pratt & Whitney PW2040 engines, the C-32B has Rolls-Royce RB211 engines. Two additional 757s are believed to be operated by the USAF in support of the US State Department's Foreign and Domestic Emergency Support Teams (FEST/DEST) under the designation C-32B.

A C-32A of the 89th AW. USAF/Samuel King

Squadron	Location	Aircraft	Wing/Group	Command	Tail code
1st AS	JB Andrews-NAF Washington, Maryland	C-32A	89th AW/OG	AMC	
486th FLTS	Eglin AFB, Florida	C-32B	AFMC	AFMC	
Air National Guard units					
150th SOS (see note 1)	JB McGuire-Dix-Lakehurst, New Jersey	C-32B	108th Wing/OG	AFSOC	
1	AFSOC-gained squadron is assigned to AMC-gained wing.				

C-40B/C Clipper

The USAF's C-40B fleet is based on the 737-7DM BBJ version of the Boeing Business Jet, but the hybrid features the 737-800's strengthened wing and landing gear. The Clippers first entered service with the 89th Airlift Wing (AW) at Andrews AFB, Maryland, in January 2003. They are operated by a crew of 11 and can carry up to 26 passengers in support of global operations. Although similar to the US Navy's C-40As the aircraft feature a VIP interior, winglets, and extended range fuel tanks that combine to provide intercontinental range, but they are not equipped to carry cargo. Additionally, the C-40Bs are equipped with secure and non-secure voice and data capabilities that include wireless local area network (LAN) and internet access and a direct-broadcast satellite television capability. Four C-40Bs are assigned to the 1st Airlift Squadron (AS) at Andrews, the 65th AS at Joint Base Pearl Harbor-Hickam, Hawaii and the 76th AS at Ramstein Air Base, Germany, and are primarily tasked as support aircraft for unified combatant commanders.

A C-40B of the 89th Airlift Wing.
USAF/Heide Couch

Squadron	Location	Aircraft	Wing/Group	Command	Tail code
1st AS	JB Andrews-NAF Washington, Maryland	C-40B	89th AW/OG	AMC	
54th AS (see note 1)	Scott AFB, Illinois	C-40C	375th AW/OG	AMC	
65th AS	JB Pearl Harbor-Hickam, Hawaii	C-40B	15th Wing/OG	PACAF	
76th AS	Ramstein AB, Germany	C-40B	86th AW/OG	USAFE	
Air National Guard units					
201st AS (see note 2)	JB Andrews-NAF Washington, Maryland	C-40C	113th Wing/OG	AMC	
Air Force Reserve Command units					
73rd AS	Scott AFB, Illinois	C-40C	932nd AW/OG	AMC	
1	Active associate squadron shares C-40C aircraft with AFRC's 932nd AW.				
2	Wing is ACC-gained.				

A C-37A of the 76th AS. USAF

Squadron	Location	Aircraft	Wing/Group	Command	Tail code
65th AS	JB Pearl Harbor-Hickam, Hawaii	C-37A	15th Wing/OG	PACAF	
76th AS	Ramstein AB, Germany	C-37A	86th AW/OG	USAFE	
99th AS	JB Andrews-NAF Washington, Maryland	C-37A/B	89th AW/OG	AMC	
310th AS (see note 1)	MacDill AFB, Florida	C-37A	6th AMW/OG	AMC	
1	Aircraft are operated in support of USCENTCOM and USSOUTHCOM.				

C-37A/B Gulfstream V/550

The USAF selected the Gulfstream V as the winner of its VC-X competition in April 1997. It initially ordered two aircraft under a $70-million contract that included options for up to four additional aircraft. Due to the significant differences between the Gulfstream V and the earlier Gulfstream IIIs and IVs that were already on the USAF inventory, the new model was assigned the military designation C-37A. Seven additional C-37As were eventually acquired along with three Gulfstream 550s that received the designation C-37B.

Providing priority airlift for senior government and military officials, the fleet of nine C-37As and three C-37Bs operates from four locations. The C-37A and C-37B are respectively powered by two BMW/Rolls-Royce BR710A1-10 or -710C4-11 turbofans and offer a maximum range of 5,800nm (10,742km) and 6,750nm (12,501km).

The USAF is moving forward with its plan to 'cross-deck' its Compass Call electronic warfare suite from the EC-130H to new Gulfstream G550 airframes and it expects to receive the first EC-X airborne electronic attack aircraft from L3 Technologies in 2021. The service is planning to replace its fleet of 14 EC-130Hs with 10 G550s that will receive the equipment as part of a 're-host' program. L-3 Technologies is responsible for the effort. The EC-X will use the airframe of the G550 airborne early warning derivative for the Compass Call program.

Squadron	Location	Aircraft	Wing/Group	Command	Tail code
Det 1, 418th FLTS	King County International Airport/Boeing Field, Seattle, Washington	KC-46A	412th TW/OG	AFMC	
56th ARS	Altus AFB, Oklahoma	(KC-46A)	97th AMW/OG	AETC	
Air Force Reserve Command units					
924th ARS (see note 1)	McConnell AFB, Kansas	(KC-46A)	931st ARW/OG	AMC	
1	Associate unit shares aircraft assigned to the 22nd ARW.				

KC-46A Pegasus

After a protracted and contentious competition, the USAF selected the Boeing KC-46 as the winner of its KC-X project in February 2011. It awarded the contractor a $3.5-billion engineering and manufacturing development (EMD) contract that included the production of four developmental KC-46A aircraft. Based on the 767-2C commercial freighter, the KC-46A will primarily be tasked with the aerial refueling mission but will also be capable of carrying passengers and cargo, and of operating in the aeromedical airlift role.

The Pegasus will be operated by a crew of three, comprising a pilot, co-pilot and boom operator. Powered by two Pratt & Whitney PW4062 engines, its airframe is 6.5ft (1.98m) longer than the standard 767-200ER series and it has a maximum take-off weight of 415,000lb (188,240kg).

The KC-46A's maximum fuel capacity is 212,299lb (96,297kg). It has an air refueling receptacle that provides the capability to on-load fuel at a rate of 1,200 gallons per minute (gpm; 4,542 liters per minute). A cargo door will allow the Pegasus to carry up to 18 cargo pallets and 58 passengers. It will transport as many as 114 passengers or 58 medical patients comprising 24 litters and 34 ambulatories during contingency operations. Its multi-point refueling system is equipped with a digital fly-by-wire boom capable of offloading fuel at a rate of 1,200gpm (4,542 liters per minute), as well as a permanent centerline drogue system and removable wing-mounted air refueling pods that can each deliver fuel at a rate of 400gpm (1,514 liters per minute). The refueling system is controlled from the crew compartment via the aerial refueling operator station (AROS) and a series of cameras on the fuselage that provide a 185° field of view. Another camera installed on the boom will capture three-dimensional video.

The first EMD aircraft conducted its maiden flight in 767-2LK freighter configuration in December 2014. The initial fully configured tanker flew when the second developmental aircraft took to the air at Paine Field in Everett on September 25, 2015.

Boeing is developing the tanker under a $4.9-billion fixed-price contract but has already absorbed around $1.65 billion in additional cost over-runs due to development and certification delays. The contractor recently received a $2.1-billion contract for the third low-rate initial production (LRIP) lot of KC-46As. The deal for 15 aircraft brings total orders for the Pegasus to 34. Boeing received a contract for the first two LRIP lots of KC-46As, which respectively included seven and 12 aircraft, in August 2016.

Training for Pegasus crews will be conducted at Altus Air Force Base, Oklahoma, by the 97th Air Mobility Wing (AMW)'s 56th Air Refueling Squadron, which will serve as the Formal Training Unit (FTU).

Up to 10 main operating bases (MOBs) will be selected for the KC-46 fleet. In 2013, the USAF announced that the first operational KC-46As would be assigned to the 22nd Air Refueling Wing (ARW) at McConnell Air Force Base in Wichita, Kansas. Delivery of the first tankers to McConnell is now expected to begin in spring 2018. A second operating base will be established at Pease Air National Guard Base, New Hampshire. The first Air Force Reserve Command-assigned tankers will be flown by the 916th ARW at Seymour Johnson AFB, North Carolina. The wing will receive the first of 12 examples beginning in the second quarter of Fiscal 2020.

The USAF has named Joint Base McGuire-Dix-Lakehurst, New Jersey and Travis AFB, California as the preferred location for the next two KC-46A MOBs. The 305th AMW will receive the first of a planned fleet of 24 tankers during Fiscal 2021. The 60th AMW will follow suit in Fiscal 2023 when the initial examples of 24 aircraft arrive at Travis.

The USAF plans to purchase 179 KC-46As and Boeing will deliver 70 by the end of 2020. It expects to sustain steady state production of 15 KC-46s a year throughout the Future Years Defense Program (FYDP).

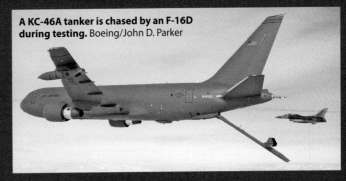

A KC-46A tanker is chased by an F-16D during testing. Boeing/John D. Parker

C-130H Hercules

Since the C-130A entered service in 1956 the USAF has operated numerous variants of the Hercules. The C-130H is the oldest of the transport versions still in service and 188 are operational in four basic versions. The last active-duty C-130Hs that were stationed in Japan were retired in October 2017.

Primarily tasked with tactical intra-theater missions, the Hercules can operate from unimproved landing strips and air-drop troops and equipment into hostile areas. The cargo variants also perform aeromedical airlift and firefighting. Powered by four Allison T56-A-15 turboprop engines, the C-130H was adapted for numerous missions that include combat search and rescue, weather reconnaissance, special operations airlift and electronic warfare, and as an aerial gunship. Specialized ski-equipped derivatives support operations in the Arctic and Antarctic.

The HC-130N/P and MC-130P/H variants are capable of refueling rotary-wing and tilt-rotor aircraft in-flight and support combat search and rescue (CSAR) and special operations missions. Although the last AFSOC MC-130P Combat Shadows were retired in May 2015, four examples are still operated by ANG. Likewise, Air Combat Command retired its final HC-130N/P Combat Kings in September 2015. The HC-130P remains in service with the ANG, but the last original HC-130Ns were retired by the AFRC in August 2017. Those aircraft were however replaced by newer HC-130H(N) airframes that had been operated by Alaska Air National Guard, which is receiving new HC-130Js.

AFSOC began phasing out its MC-130H Combat Talon IIs in September 2015; three have been placed in storage at Davis-Monthan AFB, Arizona. The MC-130H has a terrain-following/terrain-avoidance (TF/TA) radar, advanced navigation systems and a high-speed, low-level aerial delivery system. The aircraft were initially intended to deliver special operations personnel and equipment into hostile territory during day or night and in adverse weather, but were later made capable of carrying aerial refueling pods. Combat Talon IIs are now operational with special operations squadrons in Florida and Japan. The fleet includes 17 MC-130Hs with three stored at Davis-Monthan AFB, Arizona.

ACC's EC-130H Compass Call is operated as an airborne tactical weapon system and tasked with jamming enemy command and control communications and radar systems. The operational fleet includes 14 Block 35 EC-130Hs that are operated by two active-duty squadrons at Davis-Monthan.

AFSOC continues to use two gunship variants based on the C-130H airframe. Although 12 C-130Hs were converted for special missions as the MC-130W Combat Spear beginning in 2006, the aircraft were subsequently modified again to gunship configuration as AC-130W Stinger IIs.

AFSOC received the first of 13 purpose-built AC-130U Spooky gunships in July 1994 and four C-130Hs were later converted to the same configuration. The first of those aircraft was retired in September 2015. AFSOC's present fleet of 10 AC-130W and 16 AC-130U gunships will be replaced by 37 AC-130Js.

A variety of upgrades are planned for the 'legacy' Hercules fleet. These include new eight-blade UTC Aerospace NP2000 propellers that were first tested in 2010. The new propellers are initially being installed on the LC-130H fleet. The H-models are in line for engine upgrades and an avionics modernization program (AMP). AMP Increment 1 will permit the aircraft to meet communication, navigation and surveillance/ air traffic management (CNS/ ATM) mandates that take effect in January 2020. AMP Increment 2 will improve the fleet's maintainability and reliability by adding a new avionics suite that includes a terrain awareness and warning system (TAWS), flight management system (FMS), and multi-function displays (MFD), as well as enhanced communications, and electrical improvements. The latter efforts will be completed by 2028.

A 192nd Airlift Squadron 'High Rollers' C-130H3.
Jamie Hunter

C-130J Hercules

Developed by Lockheed Martin as a follow-on to the C-130H, the C-130J made its maiden flight in April 1996. The Super Hercules has a digital 'glass' cockpit and each of its four Rolls-Royce AE2100D3 turboprop engines is equipped with six-blade propellers. The USAF received its first advanced C-130J in January 1999. The initial 12 aircraft were delivered with the standard-length fuselage; the first stretched C-130J-30 was rolled out in January 2001 and delivered to the Rhode Island Air National Guard that December. Subsequent deliveries have been in the C-130J-30 configuration, which features a 15ft (4.6m) fuselage stretch that provides a 30 per cent increase in useable volume for increased seating, litters, pallets or air-drop missions.

Operated by a crew of three comprising two pilots and a loadmaster, the C-130J does not require a navigator or flight engineer like the C-130H. The stretched C-130J can carry up to eight pallets, 97 litters, 128 combat troops or 92 paratroopers compared to the C-130H and shorter-fuselage C-130J, which are both capable of taking six cargo pallets, 74 litters, 16 container delivery system (CDS) bundles, 92 combat troops or 64 paratroopers. All active-duty airlift squadrons now operate the C-130J version and 110 were on the inventory at the end of Fiscal 2017, including 15 that supported AETC training efforts.

The service has an acquisition program baseline (APB) of 169 aircraft. The final purchases are planned for 2023.

Ten additional standard-length C-130J airframes were modified for weather reconnaissance missions under the designation WC-130J and another five have been configured for electronic missions as EC-130Js. Two of the original C-130J airlifters have been converted for electronic warfare missions.

The first WC-130J was delivered to the AFRC in September 1999, and the Pennsylvania Air National Guard's 193rd Special Operations Squadron accepted its first EC-130J in October 1999. The WC-130J is tasked to penetrate tropical cyclones and hurricanes to collect high-accuracy weather data from within the storm.

The Pennsylvania Air National Guard's 193rd Special Operations Wing flies three EC-130J(CS) Commando Solo and four EC-130J(SJ) Super-J aircraft. Tasked as an airborne military information support operations (MISO) broadcast platform, the EC-130J(CS) conducts information and psychological operations (PSYOPs). The EC-130J(SJ) is a 'slick' airframe tasked with 'SOF FLEX' mobility missions, which include special operations forces airlift (SOFLIFT), military freefall (MFF), joint precision air drop system (JPADS), and PSYOP leaflet drops.

The HC-130J combat rescue and MC-130J special operations models were developed under the HC/ MC-130 recapitalization program beginning in June 2008. Intended as replacements for the HC-130N/P and MC-130E/H/P, the two variants share the same airframe as the KC-130J. Planned procurement takes in 131 aircraft.

Both variants feature the enhanced cargo handling system (ECHS), higher-capacity generators, the universal aerial refueling receptacle slipway installation (UARRSI), an AN/AAS-52 EO/IR sensor, the AN/APN-241 radar, a combat systems operator (CSO) station on the flight deck and aviation survivability equipment

Squadron	Location	Aircraft	Wing/Group	Command	Tail code
Det 2, 1st SOG	Hurlburt Field, Florida	AC-130J	1st SOW	AFSOC	
1st SOS	Kadena AB, Okinawa, Japan	MC-130H	353rd SOG	AFSOC	
4th SOS	Hurlburt Field, Florida	AC-130U	1st SOW/SOG	AFSOC	
9th SOS	Cannon AFB, New Mexico	MC-130J	27th SOW/SOG	AFSOC	
14th WPS (see note 1)	Hurlburt Field, Florida	MC-130H/J, AC-130U/W	57th Wing/USAFWS	ACC	
15th SOS	Hurlburt Field, Florida	MC-130H/J	1st SOW/SOG	AFSOC	
16th SOS	Cannon AFB, New Mexico	AC-130W	27th SOW/SOG	AFSOC	
17th SOS	Kadena AB, Okinawa, Japan	MC-130J	353rd SOG	AFSOC	
19th SOS (FTU) (see note 1)	Hurlburt Field, Florida	AC-130J/U, MC-130H	492nd SOW	AFSOC	
29th WPS (see note 1)	Little Rock AFB, Arkansas	C-130H/J	57th Wing/USAFWS	ACC	
34th WPS (see note 2)	Nellis AFB, Nevada	HC-130J	57th Wing/USAFWS	ACC	FT
36th AS	Yokota AB, Japan	C-130J	374th AW/OG	PACAF	
37th AS	Ramstein AB, Germany	C-130J	86th AW/OG	USAFE	RS
39th AS	Dyess AFB, Texas	C-130J	317th AW/OG	AMC	
40th AS	Dyess AFB, Texas	C-130J	317th AW/OG	AMC	
41st AS	Little Rock AFB, Arkansas	C-130J	19th AW/OG	AMC	
41st ECS	Davis-Monthan AFB, Arizona	EC-130H	55th Wing/ECG	ACC	DM
42nd ECS (FTU) (see note 3)	Davis-Monthan AFB, Arizona	(No aircraft assigned)	55th Wing/ECG	ACC	DM
43rd ECS	Davis-Monthan AFB, Arizona	EC-130H	55th Wing/ECG	ACC	DM
61st AS	Little Rock AFB, Arkansas	C-130J	19th AW/OG	AMC	
62nd AS (FTU) (see note 4)	Little Rock AFB, Arkansas	C-130J	314th AW/OG	AETC	
67th SOS	RAF Mildenhall, Suffolk, England	MC-130J	352nd SOW/752nd SOG	AFSOC	
71st RQS	Moody AFB, Georgia	HC-130J	23rd Wing/347th RQG	ACC	FT
79th RQS	Davis-Monthan AFB, Arizona	HC-130J	23rd Wing/563rd RQG	ACC	FT
88th TES (see note 5)	Nellis AFB, Nevada	HC-130J	53rd Wing/TEG	ACC	OT
413th FLTS (see note 6)	Hurlburt Field, Florida	MC-130H, AC-130U/J	96th TW/OG	AFMC	
415th SOS SOS	Kirtland AFB, New Mexico	HC/MC-130J	58th SOW/OG	AETC	
551st SOS (FTU) (see note 7)	Cannon AFB, New Mexico	AC-130W	492nd SOW/SOG	AFSOC	
661st AESS	TSTC Airport, Waco, Texas	NEC-130H	645th AESG (see note 8)	AFMC	
Air National Guard units					
AATTC (see note 8)	Rosecrans Memorial Airport, St Joseph, Missouri	C-130H3	57th Wing/USAFWS	ACC	
102nd RQS	Francis S. Gabreski Airport/ANGB, Westhampton Beach, New York	HC-130N/P	106th RQW/OG	ACC	
109th AS	Minneapolis St Paul International Airport/ARS, Minnesota	C-130H3	133rd AW/OG	AMC	
115th AS	NB Ventura County/Point Mugu-Channel Islands ANGS, California	C-130J	146th AW/OG	AMC	
118th AS	Bradley International Airport/ANGB, Windsor Locks, Connecticut	C-130H	103rd AW/OG	AMC	
130th AS	Yeager Airport, Charleston, West Virginia	C-130H2/3	130th AW/OG	AMC	
130th RQS	Moffett Federal Airport ANGS, California	MC-130P	129th RQW/OG	ACC	CA
139th AS	Schenectady County Airport/Stratton ANGS, Scotia, New York	C-130H2, LC-130H2/3, LC-130R	109th AW/OG	AMC	
142nd AS	New Castle County Airport, Delaware	C-130H2	166th AW/OG	AMC	
143rd AS	Quonset State Airport/Holland ANGB, North Kingston, Rhode Island	C-130J	143rd AW/OG	AMC	
154th TRS (FTU)	Little Rock AFB, Arkansas	C-130H2	189th AW/OG	AETC	
156th AS (see note 9)	Charlotte Douglas International Airport, North Carolina	C-130H3	145th AW/OG	AMC	
158th AS	Savannah Hilton Head International Airport, Georgia	C-130H3	165th AW/OG	AMC	
164th AS	Mansfield Lahm Airport, Ohio	C-130H2	179th AW/OG	AMC	
165th AS	Louisville International Airport-Standiford Field, Kentucky	C-130H2	123rd AW/OG	AMC	
169th AS	General Downing-Peoria International Airport, Illinois	C-130H3	182nd AW/OG	AMC	
180th AS	Rosecrans Memorial Airport, St Joseph, Missouri	C-130H2/H2.5	139th AW/OG	AMC	
181st AS	NAS JRB Fort Worth/Carswell Field, Texas	C-130H2	136th AW/OG	AMC	
186th AS	Great Falls International Airport, Montana	C-130H	120th AW/OG	AMC	
187th AS	Cheyenne Municipal Airport, Wyoming	C-130H3	153rd AW/OG	AMC	
188th RQS (see note 10)	Kirtland AFB, New Mexico	HC-130J, MC-130J	150th SOW/SOG	AETC	
192nd AS	Reno Tahoe International Airport/May ANGB, Nevada	C-130H2/C-130H3	152nd AW/OG	AMC	
193rd SOS	Harrisburg International Airport, Pennsylvania	EC-130J	193rd SOW/SOG	AFSOC	
198th AS	Luis Muñoz Marin International Airport/Muñiz ANGB, Puerto Rico	C-130H	156th AW/OG	AMC	
211th RQS	JB Elmendorf-Richardson, Alaska	HC-130J	176th Wing/OG	PACAF	
Air Force Reserve Command units					
5th SOS (see note 11)	Hurlburt Field, Florida	AC-130U	919th SOW/SOG	AFSOC	
39th RQS	Patrick AFB, Florida	HC-130N	920th RQW/OG	ACC	FL
53rd WRS	Keesler AFB, Mississippi	WC-130J	403rd Wing/OG	AMC	
96th AS	Minneapolis-St Paul International Airport/JARS, Minnesota	C-130H3	934th AW/OG	AMC	
327th AS (see note 12)	Little Rock AFB, Arkansas	C-130J	913th AG	AMC	
357th AS	Maxwell-Gunter AFB, Alabama	C-130H2	908th AW/OG	AMC	
700th AS	Dobbins ARB, Georgia	C-130H3	94th AW/OG	AMC	
731st AS	Peterson AFB, Colorado	C-130H3	302nd AW/OG	AMC	
757th AS	Youngstown Warren Regional Airport/JARS, Ohio	C-130H2	910th AW/OG	AMC	
758th AS (see note 13)	Pittsburgh International Airport/JARS, Pennsylvania	C-130H2	911th AW/OG	AMC	
815th AS	Keesler AFB, Mississippi	C-130J	403rd Wing/OG	AMC	

1   Squadron utilizes aircraft assigned to host wing.
2   34th WPS utilizes HC-130Js operated by the 79th RQS at Davis-Monthan AFB, Arizona.
3   Squadron utilizes EC-130H assigned to the 41st and 43rd ECS in support of FTU mission.
4   C-130J training mission reassigned from the 48th AS to the 62nd AS on September 30, 2016.
5   Combat Search and Rescue Combined Task Force (CSAR/CTF). Squadron is located at Nellis AFB but HC-130J based at Davis-Monthan AFB, Arizona.
6   Utilizes aircraft assigned to host wing.
7   645th AESG is based at Wright-Patterson AFB, Ohio.
8   Utilizes aircraft assigned to the 139th Airlift Wing.
9   156th AS to transition to C-17A.
10   Associate unit conducts training alongside the active-duty 415th SOS.
11   Associate unit, shares aircraft with co-located active-duty squadron, which supports AFSOTC/19th SOS training efforts.
12   Associate unit, shares aircraft with host wing 314th AW.
13   758th AS to transition to C-17A with eight PAA.

(ASE). Incremental upgrades will provide the MC-130J with a terrain-following/terrain-avoidance radar.

The MC-130J airframe serves as the baseline for the AC-130J Ghostrider gunship, which entered flight-testing at Eglin AFB, Florida, in January 2013. The AC-130J initially had dual AN/AAS-38 EO/IR sensors, a GAU-23 30mm cannon and precision-guided munitions including the Griffin missile and the 250lb (113kg) GBU-39 Small Diameter Bomb. Plans call for the conversion of 37 MC-130Js to gunship configuration.

The Block 20 version added a 105mm cannon, a pilot helmet-mounted tactical display, and the large aircraft infra-red countermeasures (LAIRCM) system. The flight crew is increased from seven to nine personnel. Testing of the first Block 20 variant began in July 2016 at Hurlburt Field, Florida. Planned upgrades will incorporate a permanent fire control officer station, wing-mounted AGM-114 Hellfire missiles, laser-guided Small Diameter Bombs, and radio-frequency countermeasures. The AC-130J achieved initial operational capability in September 2017. USSOCOM hopes to equip the type with a high-energy laser capability and to begin tests with the directed energy weapon in 2018. As of September 30, 2017, AFSOC's fleet included eight AC-130Js and 33 MC-130Js.

A 17th Special Operations Squadron MC-130J Commando II flies during Exercise 'Talisman Saber 2017'. USAF/Capt Jessica Tait

KC-135R/T Stratotanker, NC-135W, OC-135B, RC-135S/U/V/W, TC-135W, WC-135C/W

Originally developed for Strategic Air Command, the KC-135 series is now in its seventh decade of service. The USAF purchased the first of more than 750 aerial refueling aircraft based on Boeing's Model 367-80 in 1954 and the KC-135A entered service at Castle AFB, California, in June 1957. Deliveries were completed in 1965. Currently, 344 KC-135Rs and 54 KC-135Ts are in service with active-duty units, the ANG and AFRC. Both models are powered by four General Electric F108-GE-100 (CFM56) turbofans.

A number of KC-135Rs were modified with a multi-point refueling system (MPRS) that installed Flight Refuelling Ltd (FRL) Mk32B pods under the wings. The hose and drogue air refueling pods allow the Stratotanker to refuel aircraft that are not compatible with its flying boom.

C-135B Stratolifters were modified for numerous other roles that resulted in weather reconnaissance, electronic intelligence and command post variants. The 55th Wing at Offutt AFB, Nebraska operates specialized versions that include the OC-135B, RC-135S/U/V/W, TC-135W and WC-135C/W.

Two OC-135B observation aircraft support the Open Skies treaty, which permits short-notice, unrestricted aerial observation

flights over the territory of any of the participating nations.

Three RC-135S aircraft are equipped to collect optical and electronic data on ballistic targets that are critical to arms treaty compliance verification. The Cobra Balls also support the development of US strategic defense and theater missile defense concepts. Two RC-135U Combat Sent platforms conduct strategic electronic reconnaissance primarily directed at radar signals intelligence (SIGINT), and eight RC-135V and nine RC-135W Rivet Joint aircraft perform electronic intelligence (ELINT) missions.

Single examples of the WC-135C and WC-135W Constant Phoenix aircraft carry out the atmospheric collection task in support of the Limited Nuclear Test Ban Treaty of 1963. Their mission includes collecting air samples in order to detect the presence of radioactive particles.

Three TC-135Ws support training requirements. Additionally, a single NC-135W that is assigned to AFMC assists in the development of upgrades for the Rivet Joints. Although stationed at Offutt AFB, Nebraska, the special mission aircraft are regularly detached to forward operating locations worldwide.

Whereas the RC-135s and TC-135s are powered by the same F108 engines as the tanker variants, the OC-135B, WC-135C and WC-135W all retain the original TF33 engines.

The entire '135' fleet was modified under the Block 40 Pacer-CRAG program (CRAG

standing for compass, radar and GPS), which was completed in 2001. It eliminated the navigator position from the flight deck. The KC-135 Global Air Traffic Management (GATM) program, which was completed in 2011, upgraded the communication, navigation, surveillance and air traffic management (CNS/ATM) systems in 419 C-135-family aircraft. Rockwell Collins began development of the KC-135 Block 45 program in 2009. It provides the aircraft with a new autopilot, flight director, radar altimeter and electronic engine instrument display. Block 45 testing was

completed in April 2013 and the 22nd Air Refueling Wing at McConnell AFB, Kansas flew the initial operational Block 45 mission in 2015. Modification of the entire fleet will be completed in 2025.

Field Aviation, which purchased ARINC Aerospace Systems Engineering Services in 2015, modified two KC-135s under an engineering and manufacturing contract at its facility at Will Rogers World Airport in Oklahoma City. Another 17 low-rate initial production (LRIP) alterations were carried out by the contractor, but the Oklahoma City Air Logistics Complex's 564th Aircraft Maintenance Squadron began installing the modifications in 2015.

Squadron	Location	Aircraft	Wing/Group	Command	Tail code
38th RS	Offutt AFB, Nebraska	RC-135V/W, TC-135W	55th Wing/OG	ACC	OF
45th RS	Offutt AFB, Nebraska	WC-135W, OC-135B, RC-135S/U, TC-135S	55th Wing/OG	ACC	OF
Det 45th RS	Eielson AFB, Alaska	RC-135S	55th Wing/OG	ACC	OF
50th ARS	MacDill AFB, Florida	KC-135R	6th AMW/OG	AMC	
54th ARS (FTU)	Altus AFB, Oklahoma	KC-135R	97th AMW/OG	AETC	
64th ARS (see note 1)	Pease ANGB, Portsmouth International Airport, New Hampshire	KC-135R	22nd ARW/OG	AMC	
82nd RS	Kadena AB, Okinawa	RC-135V/W	55th Wing/OG	ACC	OF
91st ARS	MacDill AFB, Florida	KC-135R/T	6th AMW/OG	AMC	
92nd ARS	Fairchild AFB, Washington	KC-135R/T	92nd ARW/OG	AMC	
93rd ARS	Fairchild AFB, Washington	KC-135R/T	92nd ARW/OG	AMC	
95th RS (see note 2)	RAF Mildenhall, Suffolk, England	RC-135V/W	55th Wing/OG	ACC	OF
Det 1, 95th RS	NSA Souda Bay AB, Crete, Greece	RC-135V/W	55th Wing/OG	ACC	OF
99th ARS (see note 3)	Birmingham-Shuttlesworth International Airport, Alabama	KC-135R	6th AMW/OG	AMC	
338th CTS (FTU)	Offutt AFB, Nebraska	(RC/WC/OC-135 training)	55th Wing/OG	ACC	OF
343rd RS	Offutt AFB, Nebraska	RC-135V/W, TC-135W	55th Wing/OG	ACC	OF
344th ARS	McConnell AFB, Kansas	KC-135R/T	22nd ARW/OG	AMC	
349th ARS	McConnell AFB, Kansas	KC-135R/R(RT)	22nd ARW/OG	AMC	
350th ARS	McConnell AFB, Kansas	KC-135R	22nd ARW/OG	AMC	
351st ARS	RAF Mildenhall, Suffolk, England	KC-135R/T	100th ARW/OG	USAFE	
384th ARS	Fairchild AFB, Washington	KC-135R	92nd ARW/OG	AMC	
418th FLTS	Edwards AFB, California	KC-135R	412th TW/OG	AFMC	
509th WPS (see note 4)	Fairchild AFB, Washington	KC-135R	57th Wing/USAFWS	ACC	
645th AESS	Majors Field Greenville Municipal Airport, Texas	NC-135W	645th AESG (see note 5)	AFMC	
906th ARS (see note 6)	Scott AFB, Illinois	KC-135R	305th AMW/OG	AMC	
909th ARS	Kadena AB, Okinawa	KC-135R	18th Wing/OG	PACAF	
911th ARS (see note 7)	Seymour Johnson AFB, North Carolina	KC-135R	6th AMW/OG	AMC	
912th ARS (see note 8)	March ARB, California	KC-135R	92nd ARW/OG	AMC	
Air National Guard units					
106th ARS	Birmingham-Shuttlesworth International Airport, Alabama	KC-135R	117th ARW/OG	AMC	
108th ARS	Scott AFB, Illinois	KC-135R	126th ARW/OG	AMC	

A RC-135V Rivet Joint of the 763rd Expeditionary Reconnaissance Squadron.
USAF/TSgt Amy M. Lovgren

Squadron	Location			
116th ARS (see note 9)	Fairchild AFB, Washington	KC-135R	141st ARW/OG	AMC
117th ARS	Forbes Field Airport, Topeka, Kansas	KC-135R	190th ARW/OG	AMC
126th ARS	Gen Mitchell International Airport/ARS, Milwaukee, Wisconsin	KC-135R	128th ARW/OG	AMC
132nd ARS	Bangor International Airport, Maine	KC-135R	101st ARW/OG	AMC
133rd ARS	Pease ANGB-Portsmouth International Airport, New Hampshire	KC-135R	157th ARW/OG	AMC
141st ARS	JB McGuire-Dix-Lakehurst, New Jersey	KC-135R	108th Wing/OG	AMC
146th ARS	Pittsburgh International Airport, Pennsylvania	KC-135T	171st ARW/OG	AMC
147th ARS	Pittsburgh International Airport, Pennsylvania	KC-135T	171st ARW/OG	AMC
151st ARS	McGhee Tyson Airport/ANGB, Knoxville, Tennessee	KC-135R	134th ARW/OG	AMC
153rd ARS	Meridian Regional Airport-Key Field, Mississippi	KC-135R	186th ARW/OG	AMC
166th ARS	Rickenbacker International Airport/ANGB, Columbus, Ohio	KC-135R	121st ARW/OG	AMC
168th ARS	Eielson AFB, Alaska	KC-135R	168th Wing/OG	PACAF
171st ARS	Selfridge ANGB, Mount Clemens, Michigan	KC-135T	127th Wing/OG	AMC
173rd ARS	Lincoln Municipal Airport/ANGB, Nebraska	KC-135R	155th ARW/OG	AMC
174th ARS	Sioux Gateway Airport/Col Bud Day Field, Sioux City, Iowa	KC-135R	185th ARW/OG	AMC
191st ARS	Roland R. Wright ANGB/Salt Lake City International Airport, Utah	KC-135R	151st ARW/OG	AMC
197th ARS	Goldwater ANGB/Phoenix Sky Harbor International Airport, Arizona	KC-135R	161st ARW/OG	AMC
203rd ARS	JB Pearl Harbor-Hickam, Hawaii	KC-135R	154th Wing/OG	PACAF
238th CTS (FTU) (see note 10)	Offutt AFB, Nebraska	RC/WC/OC-135	170th Group	ACC	OF
Air Force Reserve Command units				
18th ARS (see note 11)	McConnell AFB, Kansas	KC-135R	931st ARW/OG	AMC
63rd ARS	MacDill AFB, Florida	KC-135R	927th ARW/OG	AMC
72nd ARS	Grissom ARB, Indiana	KC-135R	434th ARW/OG	AMC
74th ARS	Grissom ARB, Indiana	KC-135R	434th ARW/OG	AMC
77th ARS	Seymour Johnson AFB, North Carolina	KC-135R	916th ARW/OG	AMC
314th ARS	Beale AFB, California	KC-135R	940th ARW/OG	AMC
328th ARS	Niagara Falls International Airport/JARS, New York	KC-135R	914th ARW/OG	AMC
336th ARS	March ARB, California	KC-135R	452nd AMW/OG	AMC
465th ARS	Tinker AFB, Oklahoma	KC-135R	507th ARW/OG	AMC
730th AMTS (see note 12)	Altus AFB, Oklahoma	KC-135R	507th ARW/OG	AETC
756th ARS	JB Andrews-NAF Washington, Maryland	KC-135R	459th ARW/OG	AMC
905th ARS (see note 11)	McConnell AFB, Kansas	KC-135R	931st ARW/OG	AMC

1 Active associate squadron shares aircraft assigned to the ANG's co-located 157th ARW.
2 95th RS will relocate to RAF Lakenheath.
3 Active associate squadron shares aircraft assigned to the ANG's co-located 117th ARW.
4 Squadron utilizes aircraft assigned to host wing.
5 645th AESG is based at Wright-Patterson AFB, Ohio.
6 Active associate squadron shares aircraft assigned to the ANG's co-located 126th ARW.
7 Active associate squadron shares aircraft assigned to the AFRC's co-located 916th ARW.
8 Active associate squadron shares aircraft assigned to the AFRC's co-located 452nd AMW.
9 Air National Guard associate unit shares aircraft assigned to the 92nd ARW.
10 Associate squadron operates alongside the 55th Wing's 338th CTS.
11 Associate unit shares aircraft assigned to the 22nd ARW.
12 Associate unit supports 97th AMW KC-135 and C-17 training operations.

A KC-135R of the 100th ARW refuels a pair of F-35As during a deployment to the UK in 2017. Jamie Hunter

C-145A Skytruck

AFSOC operates five C-145A Skytrucks. They are based on the Antonov An-28, as built by present-day Sikorsky subsidiary PZL-Mielec (Polskie Zaklady Lotnicze) in Poland. They type is also known as the Combat Coyote.

The AFSOC revealed plans to procure 10 Skytrucks in February 2009 and the aircraft were initially assigned to the multi-engine light inter-theater mobility mission. The Sierra Nevada Corporation (SNC) delivered the first aircraft to AFSOC in August 2009 to transport small special operations teams to austere airstrips. The project was later expanded to 17 aircraft and the last was delivered in March 2012. The C-145A was later reassigned to the Aviation Foreign Internal Defense (AvFID) mission and transferred from Cannon to Duke Field in Florida, the fleet being reduced. By late 2015, 11 of the surviving C-145As were retired. Nine Skytrucks remain in storage at Davis-Monthan AFB, Arizona.

Squadron	Location	Aircraft	Wing/Group	Command	Tail code
6th SOS	Duke Field, Florida	C-145A	492nd SOW/SOG	AFSOC	
Air Force Reserve Command units					
5th SOS (see note 1)	Hurlburt Field, Florida	C-145A	919th SOW/SOG	AFSOC	
711th SOS (see note 2)	Duke Field, Florida	C-145A	919th SOW/SOG	AFSOC	

1 Associate unit, shares responsibility for aircraft with co-located active-duty squadron, which supports AFSOTC/19th SOS combat aviation advisor (CAA) training efforts.
2 711th SOS operates as an associate squadron and supports the 6th SOS training mission.

A 919th Special Operations Wing C-145A drops a parachute bundle. USAF/Sam King

C-146A Wolfhound

The AFSOC operates a fleet of 20 C-146As, which are based on the Dornier 328-110 airliner. The Wolfhound is primary tasked to provide US Special Operations Command with operational movement of small teams. The twin-engine aircraft is powered by two Pratt & Whitney Canada PW119C turboprop engines and can carry up to 27 passengers, 6,000lb (2,722kg) of cargo, or up to four litter patients. Procurement began in Fiscal 2010 with service entry from October 2011.

The entire fleet has been upgraded to Block 20 configuration, featuring an NVG-compatible cockpit. Wolfhounds are deployed with multiple commands. A single 328 'Cougar' is operated as a demonstrator for ISR missions.

Squadron	Location	Aircraft	Wing/Group	Command	Tail code
524th SOS	Duke Field, Florida	C-146A	492nd SOW/SOG	AFSOC	
551st SOS (FTU) (see note 1)	Cannon AFB, New Mexico	C-146A	AFSOAWC	AFSOC	
	Wright-Patterson AFB, Ohio	328-100	645th AESG	AFMC	
Air Force Reserve Command units					
859th SOS	Hurlburt Field, Florida	C-146A	919th SOW/SOG	AFSOC	

A C-146 Wolfhound assigned to the 919th Special Operations Wing. USAF/Dan Neely

E-3B/C/G Sentry

The USAF operates 31 E-3 airborne warning and control system (AWACS) aircraft. The battle management command and control (BMC2) weapon system provides all-weather surveillance, command, control and communications to combatant commanders. The Sentry has a 30ft (9.1m) rotating radar antenna that allows its AN/APY-1/2 long-range surveillance radar to locate low-flying targets at a range of more than 200 miles (320km).

The AWACS program can be traced to July 1970 when Boeing received a contract to modify two 707-320 airframes with two competing radar systems. The aircraft flew for the first time under the designation EC-137D, in February 1972. The Westinghouse (now Northrop Grumman) AN/APY-1 radar was selected in October 1972 after flight tests were completed.

Deliveries of the initial production E-3A to Tinker AFB, Oklahoma, began in March 1977. The 26th and subsequent aircraft were equipped with the AN/APY-2 radar that provided improved maritime capabilities. The initial production E-3A was also converted to that configuration. Upgrades later standardized the aircraft, the AN/APY-1-equipped E-3As being designated as the E-3B, while those equipped with the AN/APY-2 became E-3Cs.

A passive sensor suite was added when the Sentry was equipped with the AN/AYR-1 electronic support measures system. Further modifications provided the E-3 with a GPS navigation capability, upgraded secure datalink communications and an upgraded central computer. A radar system improvement program (RSIP) replaced the radar computer and upgraded the radar operator consoles, other selected radar system hardware, and radar sub-system software. Current modernization efforts are focused on upgrading the battle management mission systems, combat identification and the cockpit avionics suite.

Known as the Block 40/45 upgrade, the $2.7-billion program is the largest in the history of the AWACS. It replaces the mission computing system with open-architecture, commercial off-the-shelf (COTS) hardware that includes new mission computing hardware and software, mission consoles, and upgraded electronic support measures equipment. The first E-3G was rolled out in August 2011 and the new model achieved initial operational capability in July 2015.

It was deployed to South-west Asia for the first time in November 2015. As of October 2017, the USAF had received 16 E-3Gs. Conversion of the last of 31 aircraft should be completed by 2020.

The 552nd Air Control Wing at Tinker received the first Sentry updated under the Diminishing manufacturing sources Replacement of Avionics for Global Operations and Navigation (DRAGON) program in January 2017. The upgrade provides cockpit avionics modifications that replace analog dials with five modern digital multi-color 'glass' displays and installs a new weather radar. This will eliminate the need for a navigator, reducing the flight crew from four to three. The upgrades ensure that the Sentry complies with future air traffic control requirements in reduced-vertical separation minimum airspace and optimal flight levels, increasing fuel efficiency and reducing clearance delays. The entire Sentry fleet should receive the DRAGON mods by the fourth quarter of Fiscal 2025.

E-3s are in service with seven active USAF squadrons and a single AFRC associate squadron. The USAF expects to retain the E-3G in service until 2035 and is considering its plans for replacing the platform. Its advanced battle management and surveillance (ABMS) system is expected to provide an evolutionary leap in capability over the Sentry.

Squadron	Location	Aircraft	Wing/Group	Command	Tail code
960th AACS	Tinker AFB, Oklahoma	E-3B/C/G	552nd ACW/OG	ACC	OK
961st AACS	Kadena AB, Okinawa	E-3B/C	18th Wing/OG	PACAF	ZZ
962nd AACS	JB Elmendorf-Richardson, Alaska	E-3B/C	3rd Wing/OG	PACAF	AK
963rd AACS	Tinker AFB, Oklahoma	E-3G	552nd ACW/OG	ACC	OK
964th AACS	Tinker AFB, Oklahoma	E-3G	552nd ACW/OG	ACC	OK
965th AACS	Tinker AFB, Oklahoma	E-3G	552nd ACW/OG	ACC	OK
966th AACS (FTU)	Tinker AFB, Oklahoma	E-3G	552nd ACW/OG	ACC	OK
Det 1, 605th TES (see note 1)	Tinker AFB, Oklahoma	E-3B/C/G	505th CCW/TEG	ACC	OK
Air Force Reserve Command units					
970th AACS (see note 2)	Tinker AFB, Oklahoma	E-3G	513th ACG	ACC	OK

1   605th TES and 505th CCW are located at Hurlburt Field, Florida. 505th TEG is located at Nellis AFB, Nevada and conducts operational test of ISR weapons systems.
2   Unit operates E-3B/C/G as an associate to the 552nd ACW.

USAF E-3s are constantly deployed and play a vital role in the current Operation 'Inherent Resolve'. USAF

E-4B 'Nightwatch'

The USAF operates four modified Boeing 747-200Bs that are tasked as the National Airborne Operations Center (NAOC) for the National Command Authorities (NCA). The first aircraft entered service with Strategic Air Command under the designation E-4A in December 1974. The aircraft were later upgraded and the service received the first E-4B in January 1980. The last example was delivered in January 1985.

E-4Bs are intended to provide US forces with a survivable, command, control and communications center in the event of a national emergency or destruction of ground command control centers. The E-4Bs are flown by the 1st Airborne Air Control Squadron and operational control has been assigned to Air Force Global Strike Command since October 1, 2016. The aircraft execute emergency war orders, but in the event of natural emergencies are also tasked to support the Federal Emergency Management Agency (FEMA) by co-ordinating the actions of civil authorities.

One E-4B and a crew of 63 personnel are generally on 24-hour ground alert, to provide direct support for the NCA. Its crew can include as many as 114 personnel, comprising a joint-service operations team, a flight crew, a maintenance and security component, and a communications team.

Ongoing upgrades will provide the aircraft with advanced extremely high-frequency (AEHF) compatibility and the low-frequency transmit system (LFTS). The USAF's Fiscal Year 2018 budget request included funds to continue the initial research, development, test and evaluation efforts associated with a NAOC recapitalization program.

Squadron	Location	Aircraft	Wing/Group	Command	Tail code
1st ACCS	Offutt AFB, Nebraska	E-4B	595th CACG	ACC	

An E-4B of the 1st ACCS visits Travis AFB.
USAF/SSgt Nicole Leidholm

E-8C Joint STARS

The USAF operates a fleet of 16 E-8C Joint Surveillance and Target Acquisition Radar System — Joint STARS (JSTARS) airborne battle management command and control (BMC2) aircraft based at Robins AFB, Georgia.

JSTARS development began in September 1985 when Grumman Aerospace received a contract for two E-8A test aircraft. The C2ISR system uses synthetic aperture radar (SAR) and ground moving target indicator (GMTI) modes to provide long-endurance, all-weather surveillance and targeting of moving and stationary targets. The radar was initially installed in two pre-owned, refurbished, Boeing 707-300-series airliners. The first of those carried out its maiden flight in December 1988. The E-8 made its debut deployment during Operation 'Desert Storm' in 1991, while still under development.

A single E-8C development aircraft followed in 1994, with a subsequent 17 production aircraft. Like the developmental platform, the host aircraft is a remanufactured 707-300. The E-8C features a 40ft (12m)-long, canoe-shaped radome under the forward fuselage that houses the AN/APY-7 radar's 24ft (7.3m), side-looking phased array antenna. The antenna provides a 120° field of view covering nearly 19,305 square miles (50,000 square km) and the system can detect targets at ranges from 31 to 155 miles (50 to 250km) from the aircraft.

The first operational E-8C arrived at Robins AFB in June 1996 and the last was delivered in April 2005. Since entering service, one E-8C has been written off as a result of a ground fire. A single TE-8A supports flight crew training.

In January 2014, the USAF announced plans to develop a replacement for the E-8C. During

An E-8C of the 116th Air Control Wing, at Robins AFB. USAF/Greg L. Davis

August 2015, the USAF issued pre-engineering and manufacturing development (EMD) contracts associated with the JSTARS recap program to Northrop Grumman, Lockheed Martin and Boeing. The following March, the USAF awarded Northrop Grumman Electronic Systems (NGES) and Raytheon Space and Airborne Systems (RSAS) sole-source contracts to mature related radar designs. Replacement of the E-8C is expected to cost around $6.9 billion.

The USAF issued the final RFP for the recap program in December 2016. At that time the service expected to award a contract during Fiscal 2018 with the new aircraft achieving initial operational capability by 2024. According to the RFP, the effort will include three EMD JSTARS recap systems. In addition to the test aircraft the contract will include options for two

low-rate initial production (LRIP) aircraft and full-rate production of four aircraft in each of three annual lots.

Teamed with Raytheon and Bombardier, Lockheed Martin offered a variant of the Global 6000 business jet, which would be equipped with Raytheon's Skynet active electronically scanned array (AESA) long-range, ground surveillance radar. Northrop Grumman's team includes Gulfstream Aerospace and L-3 Communication, and its offer is based on Gulfstream's G550. Boeing proposed a modified version of its 737-700 commercial airliner.

More recently, the USAF revealed that it is re-examining its plans for replacing the JSTARS. It was expected to make a final decision in October 2017, but an announcement has now been pushed out to early 2018.

Squadron	Location	Aircraft	Wing/Group	Command	Tail code
12th ACCS (see Note 1)	Robins AFB, Georgia	E-8C	461st ACW/OG	ACC	GA
16th ACCS (see Note 1)	Robins AFB, Georgia	E-8C	461st ACW/OG	ACC	GA
330th CTS (FTU) (see Note 1)	Robins AFB, Georgia	TE-8A, E-8C	461st ACW/OG	ACC	GA
Det 2, 605th TES (See Note 2)	Melbourne International Airport, Florida	E-8C	505th CCW/TEG	ACC	
Air National Guard units					
128th ACCS	Robins AFB, Georgia	E-8C	116th ACW/OG	ACC	GA

1   Active associate squadron utilizes aircraft assigned to the Georgia Air National Guard's 116th ACW.
2   605th TES and 505th CCW are s located at Hurlburt Field, Florida. 505th TEG is located at Nellis AFB, Nevada and conducts Operational Test of ISR weapons systems.

E-9A 'Widget'

Air Combat Command's 53rd Weapon Evaluation Group's 82nd Aerial Targets Squadron operates a pair of highly modified de Havilland Canada DHC-8 aircraft under the designation E-9A. Modified by Sierra Research, the Dash 8s entered service as range support aircraft in 1988 and

are assigned to the 82nd Aerial Targets Squadron, at Tyndall AFB, Florida. Known as 'Widgets', the E-9As are equipped with an AN/APS-143(V)1 airborne sea surveillance radar and a phased array antenna that can simultaneously receive, record and downlink telemetry from aircraft, missiles and other sources.

The E-9As are assigned to the 82nd ATRS. USAF/MSgt Michael Ammons

Squadron	Location	Aircraft	Wing/Group	Command	Tail code
82nd ATRS	Tyndall AFB, Florida	E-9A	53rd Wing/53rd WEG	ACC	TD

E-11A

Initially installed aboard Bombardier BD700 Global Express test aircraft N901GX, the Battlefield Airborne Communications Node (BACN) was developed by Northrop Grumman.

The system relays voice communications over long distances, acting as an airborne data relay and gateway that allows real-time information to be passed between tactical datalink

systems. BACN was initially integrated on two Global Express XRS aircraft that were deployed to Afghanistan in late 2008. Increased to three aircraft, USAF purchased them outright in 2011 and the designation E-11A was assigned. Northrop Grumman produced a fourth in late 2013. The E-11A flew its 10,000th sortie from Kandahar on February 24, 2017. The system is also carried by Block 20 EQ-4B remotely piloted aircraft.

An E-11A awaits its next mission at Kandahar Airfield, Afghanistan. USAF

Squadron	Location	Aircraft	Wing/Group	Command	Tail code
430th EECS	Kandahar Airport, Afghanistan	E-11A	451st EOG/AEG	ACC	

An F-15E Strike Eagle of the 492nd Expeditionary Fighter Squadron. USAF/SSgt Michael Battles

Squadron	Location	Aircraft	Wing/Group	Command	Tail code
550th FS	Klamath Falls Airport-Kingsley Field, Oregon	F-15C/D	56th FW/OG	AETC	
17th WPS	Nellis AFB, Nevada	F-15E	57th Wing/USAFWS	ACC	WA
40th FLTS	Eglin AFB, Florida	F-15C/D/E	96th TW/OG	AFMC	ET
44th FS	Kadena AB, Okinawa	F-15C/D	18th Wing/OG	PACAF	ZZ
67th FS	Kadena AB, Okinawa	F-15C/D	18th Wing/OG	PACAF	ZZ
85th TES	Eglin AFB, Florida	F-15C/E	53rd Wing/53rd TEG	ACC	OT
333rd FS (FTU)	Seymour Johnson AFB, North Carolina	F-15E	4th FW/OG	ACC	SJ
334th FS (FTU)	Seymour Johnson AFB, North Carolina	F-15E	4th FW/OG	ACC	SJ
335th FS	Seymour Johnson AFB, North Carolina	F-15E	4th FW/OG	ACC	SJ
336th FS	Seymour Johnson AFB, North Carolina	F-15E	4th FW/OG	ACC	SJ
389th FS	Mountain Home AFB, Idaho	F-15E	366th FW/OG	ACC	MO
391st FS	Mountain Home AFB, Idaho	F-15E	366th FW/OG	ACC	MO
422nd TES	Nellis AFB, Nevada	F-15C/D/E	53rd Wing/53rd TEG	ACC	OT
428th FS (see note 1)	Mountain Home AFB, Idaho	F-15SG	366th FW/OG	ACC	MO
433rd WPS (see note 2)	Nellis AFB, Nevada	F-15C/D	57th Wing/USAFWS	ACC	WA
492nd FS	RAF Lakenheath, Suffolk, England	F-15E	48th FW/OG	USAFE	LN
493rd FS	RAF Lakenheath, Suffolk, England	F-15C/D	48th FW/OG	USAFE	LN
494th FS	RAF Lakenheath, Suffolk, England	F-15E	48th FW/OG	USAFE	LN
Air National Guard units					
114th FS	Klamath Falls Airport-Kingsley Field, Oregon	F-15C/D	173rd FW/OG	AETC	
122nd FS	NAS JRB New Orleans, Louisiana	F-15C/D	159th FW/OG	ACC	JZ
123rd FS	Portland International Airport/ANGB, Oregon	F-15C/D	142nd FW/OG	ACC	
131st FS	Westfield Barnes Airport/ANGB, Massachusetts	F-15C/D	104th FW/OG	ACC	MA
159th FS	Jacksonville International Airport, Florida	F-15C/D	125th FW/OG	ACC	
194th FS	Fresno-Yosemite International Airport/ANGB, California	F-15C/D	144th FW/OG	ACC	
Air Force Reserve Command units					
84 TES (see Note 3)	Eglin AFB, Florida	F-15C/E	926th Wing/OG	ACC	OT
307th FS (see Note 3)	Seymour Johnson AFB, North Carolina	F-15E	944th FW/414th FG	ACC	SJ
706th FS (see Note 3)	Nellis AFB, Nevada	F-15C/D/E	926th Wing/OG	ACC	WA

1 428th FS trains Republic of Singapore Air Force pilots.
2 Squadron utilizes aircraft assigned to host wing.
3 Classic associate squadron utilizes aircraft assigned to host wing.

F-15C/D Eagle, F-15E Strike Eagle

Although the first F-15s entered service at Luke AFB, Arizona in November 1974, the Eagle continues to be an important component of the USAF fleet. In fact, the service plans to retain nearly F-15C/Ds in service until at least 2040. Planned offensive and defensive upgrades will ensure that the type remains capable and able to survive in current and future threat environments. The upgrades will also allow the fighters to operate alongside the F-22A and F-35A.

The plans replace the original mechanically scanned radar systems, installed in 179 F-15Cs, with Raytheon AN/APG-63(V)3 active electronically scanned array (AESA) radars. The aircraft are receiving a more robust and powerful datalink and the Eagle passive/active warning

survivability system (EPAWSS) will replace the earlier AN/ALQ-135 tactical electronic warfare system (TEWS). The integrated electronic attack suite incorporates a digital radar warning receiver, digital radio frequency memory jammer and AN/ALE-58 BOL advanced countermeasures dispenser. Additionally, the F-15C's current mission computer will be replaced by the Advanced Display Core Processor (ADCP) II in 179 aircraft. The new processor will support future upgrades such as data fusion connectivity with other fighters including the F-22A and F-35A. The upgrade also installs a new high-resolution color display in place of the fighter's current vertical situation display (VSD).

The USAF recently selected Lockheed Martin's Legion Pod Infra-red search and track (IRST) system for the F-15C fleet. The service plans to acquire 130 such systems for integration. Delivery

of the pods will begin in 2018 and Legion will achieve initial operational capability (IOC) in 2020. The passive capability is felt vital for operations in contested environments.

The fleet today includes 212 F-15Cs and 23 F-15Ds that were initially fielded in 1979. The bulk

of the fighters are assigned to ANG units, but 75 are flown by operational PACAF and USAFE squadrons and ACC training/test units.

The multi-role F-15E Strike Eagle first flew in December 1986 and the current fleet includes 218 aircraft. The Strike Eagles are getting upgrades that include the Raytheon AN/APG-82(V)1 AESA radar, which is being installed in place of the original AN/APG-70. The 366th Fighter Wing at Mountain Home AFB, Idaho, received the first F-15E so equipped in June 2014. Installation of the EPAWSS will increase survivability in high-threat environments and allow the Strike Eagle to counter current and future air-to-air and ground-to-air and infra-red threats. Fielding will begin in 2018. Additionally, 219 ADCP II/VSD installations are planned for the F-15E fleet.

F-15Cs of the 122nd Fighter Squadron, Louisiana ANG. Jamie Hunter

F-16Cs of the 20th FW fly in formation as part of a commemoration of the 100th anniversary of the 55th Fighter Squadron.
USAF/TSgt Gregory Brook

F-16C/D
Fighting Falcon

Originally developed by General Dynamics as the Model 401, under the USAF's Lightweight Fighter (LWF) program, the YF-16 first flew in February 1974. The fighter was later selected to fulfill the USAF's Air Combat Fighter (ACF) requirement. The initial F-16A first flew in December 1976 and deliveries to Luke AFB, Arizona, began in August 1978. Between 1978 and 2005 the USAF accepted 2,231 F-16s from General Dynamics and Lockheed Martin, which purchased the former's Fort Worth division in 1993.

With 941 F-16C/Ds in service, the Fighting Falcon — or 'Viper' — remains the service's primary multi-role fighter and comprises 50 per cent of the USAF fleet. Although the inventory is primarily composed of Block 30/32, 40/42 and 50/52 models, a small number of older Block 25s continue to support test and training missions. ANG units operate more than 330 Block 25/30/32/40/42/50/52 F-16C/Ds. Hill AFB, Utah received the first operational F-16A in January 1979.

Production switched to the Block 25 F-16, which was first delivered in July 1984. The Block 30/40 and 32/42 are respectively powered by the General Electric F110-GE-100 and the F100-PW-220. Block 40/42 aircraft were the first capable of carrying the LANTIRN AN/AAQ-13 navigation and AN/AAQ-14 targeting pods. Block 50/52s were respectively powered by F110-GE-129 and F100-PW-229 Improved Performance Engines. Block 50D/52D jets were equipped with the HARM avionics/launcher interface computer (ALIC) and the AN/ASQ-213 HARM Targeting System (HTS) that provided a fully autonomous employment capability for the AGM-88 missile and allowed the aircraft to operate in the 'Wild Weasel' suppression of enemy air defenses role.

The entire fleet has received multiple upgrades including the Common Configuration Implementation Program (CCIP), which provided enhanced mission capabilities and integrated a common avionics configuration on Block 40/42 and 50/52 fighters. Between 2002 and 2011 more than 200 Block 50/52 and 420 Block 40/42 jets received the CCIP modifications. The project provided a new avionics suite that included a modular mission computer, color displays, common missile warning systems, advanced datalink IFF systems and the Joint Helmet-Mounted Cueing System (JHMCS). F-16s are compatible with a variety of precision laser- and GPS-guided weapons as well as AN/AAQ-28 Litening and AN/AAQ-33 Sniper targeting pods.

Future plans call for a service-life extension program (SLEP) that will extend the airframe structural service lives of 300 aircraft from the current 8,000 hours to 12,000 hours. This will allow the USAF to operate the upgraded fighters until 2048 or beyond. The Air Force recently awarded Northrop Grumman a $244-million contract to provide 72 AN/APG-83 scalable agile beam radar (SABR) active electronically scanned array (AESA) systems that will replace the type's AN/APG-68 mechanically scanned radar. The AESA will initially be installed on Air National Guard F-16Cs that conduct the air defense mission. The ANG fighters make up 56 per cent of the nation's aerospace control alert (ACA) fighter force. A more comprehensive radar modernization program for as many as 300 F-16Cs is being considered as a 'new start' program in 2018. Initial fielding under that effort would begin in 2022. As of September 30, 2017, the USAF fleet comprised 786 F-16Cs and 155 F-16Ds.

The F-16 was selected as a replacement for the QF-4 full-scale aerial target (FSAT). Two Block 15 F-16As, two Block 25 and two Block 30 F-16Cs were initially modified by Boeing Global Services and Support to QF-16 configuration. The first QF-16 was delivered to Tyndall AFB, Florida, for operational and developmental testing in November 2012. Low-rate initial production (LRIP) began in late 2013 and the first production QF-16C was delivered to the 82nd Aerial Targets Squadron at Tyndall on March 11, 2015. The FSAT achieved initial operational capability at the Florida base on September 23, 2016, when 15 QF-16s were available to support operations. QF-16s are operational at Tyndall and Holloman AFB, New Mexico.

Squadron	Location	Aircraft	Wing/Group	Command	Tail code
Det 1, 56th OG	Tucson International Airport, Arizona	F-16C/D	56th FW/OG	AETC	AZ
AATC	Tucson International Airport, Arizona	F-16C/D (Block 32)	57th Wing/USAFWS	ACC	AT
USAF ADS	Nellis AFB, Nevada	F-16C/D (Block 52)	57th Wing	ACC	
USAF TPS	Edwards AFB, California	NF-16D	412th TW/OG	AFMC	
8th FS	Holloman AFB, New Mexico	F-16C/D (Block 40)	56th FW/54th FG	AETC	HO
13th FS	Misawa AB, Japan	F-16C/D (Block 50)	35th FW/OG	PACAF	WW
14th FS	Misawa AB, Japan	F-16C/D (Block 50)	35th FW/OG	PACAF	WW
16th WPS	Nellis AFB, Nevada	F-16C (Block 42/52), F-16D (Block 52)	57th Wing/USAFWS	ACC	WA
18th AGRS	Eielson AFB, Alaska	F-16C/D (Block 30)	354th FW/OG	PACAF	AK
21st FS (see note 1)	Luke AFB, Arizona	F-16A/B (Block 20)	56th FW/OG	AETC	LF
35th FS	Kunsan AB, Republic of Korea	F-16C/D (Block 40)	8th FW/OG	PACAF	WP
36th FS	Osan AB, Republic of Korea	F-16C/D (Block 50)	51st FW/OG	PACAF	OS
40th FLTS	Eglin AFB, Florida	F-16C (Block 25/40/42/50), F-16D (Block 40/50)	96th TW/OG	AFMC	ET
55th FS	Shaw AFB, South Carolina	F-16C/D (Block 50)	20th FW/OG	ACC	SW
64th AGRS	Nellis AFB, Nevada	F-16C/D (Block 25/32/42)	57th Wing/57th ATG	ACC	WA
77th FS	Shaw AFB, South Carolina	F-16C/D (Block 50)	20th FW/OG	ACC	SW
79th FS	Shaw AFB, South Carolina	F-16C/D (Block 50)	20th FW/OG	ACC	SW
80th FS	Kunsan AB, Republic of Korea	F-16C/D (Block 40)	8th FW/OG	PACAF	WP
82nd ATRS	Tyndall AFB, Florida	QF-16A/C	53rd Wing/53rd WEG	ACC	TD
85th TES	Eglin AFB, Florida	F-16C/D (Block 40/50), QF-16C	53rd Wing/53rd TEG	ACC	OT
309th FS	Luke AFB, Arizona	F-16C/D (Block 25)	56th FW/OG	AETC	LF
310th FS	Luke AFB, Arizona	F-16C/D (Block 42)	56th FW/OG	AETC	LF
311th FS	Holloman AFB, New Mexico	F-16C/D (Block 42)	56th FW/54th OG	AETC	LF
314th FS	Holloman AFB, New Mexico	F-16C/D (Block 42)	56th FW/54th OG	AETC	LF
315th FS (see note 2)	Burlington International Airport, Vermont	F-16C (Block 30)	20th FW/495th FG	ACC	
316th FS (see note 2)	McEntire JNGS, Eastover, South Carolina	F-16C (Block 52)	20th FW/495th FG	ACC	
355th FS (see note 2)	NAS JRB Fort Worth, Texas	F-16C (Block 30)	20th FW/495th FG	ACC	TX
367th FS (see note 2)	Homestead ARB, Florida	F-16C (Block 30)	20th FW/495th FG	ACC	FM
377th FS (see note 2)	Montgomery Regional Airport-Dannelly Field, Alabama	F-16C (Block 30)	20th FW/495th FG	ACC	AL
378th FS (see note 2)	Dane County Regional Airport-Truax Field, Madison, Wisconsin	F-16C (Block 30)	20th FW/495th FG	ACC	WI

Squadron	Location	Aircraft	Wing/Group	Command	Tail code
416th FLTS	Edwards AFB, California	F-16C/D (Block 30/40/42/50)	412th TW/OG	AFMC	ED
422nd TES	Nellis AFB, Nevada	F-16C/D (Block 42/52)	53rd Wing/53rd TEG	ACC	OT
425th FS (see note 3)	Luke AFB, Arizona	F-16C/D (Block 42)	56th FW/OG	AETC	LF
480th FS	Spangdahlem AB, Germany	F-16C/D (Block 50)	52nd FW/OG	USAFE	SP
510th FS	Aviano AB, Italy	F-16C/D (Block 40)	31st FW/OG	USAFE	AV
555th FS	Aviano AB, Italy	F-16C/D (Block 40)	31st FW/OG	USAFE	AV
Air National Guard units					
100th FS	Montgomery Regional Airport-Dannelly Field, Alabama	F-16C/D (Block 30)	187th FW/OG	ACC	AL
112th FS	Toledo Express Airport, Swanton, Ohio	F-16C/D (Block 42)	180th FW/OG	ACC	OH
119th FS	Atlantic City International Airport/ANGB, New Jersey	F-16C (Block 30)	177th FW/OG	ACC	NJ
120th FS	Buckley AFB, Aurora, Colorado	F-16C (Block 30)	140th FW/OG	ACC	CO
121st FS	JB Andrews-NAF Washington, Maryland	F-16C/D (Block 30)	113th Wing/OG	ACC	DC
125th FS	Tulsa International Airport, Oklahoma	F-16C/D (Block 42)	138th FW/OG	ACC	OK
134th FS	Burlington International Airport, Vermont	F-16C (Block 30)	158th FW/OG	ACC	
148th FS (FTU) (see note 4)	Tucson International Airport, Arizona	F-16A/B (MLU)	162nd Wing/OG	AETC	AZ
152nd FS (FTU)	Tucson International Airport, Arizona	F-16C/D (Block 42)	162nd Wing/OG	AETC	AZ
157th FS	McEntire JNGS, Eastover, South Carolina	F-16C/D (Block 52)	169th FW/OG	ACC	
175th FS	Sioux Falls Regional Airport-Joe Foss Field, South Dakota	F-16C/D (Block 40)	114th FW/OG	ACC	
176th FS	Dane County Regional Airport-Truax Field, Madison, Wisconsin	F-16C (Block 30)	115th FW/OG	ACC	WI
179th FS	Duluth International Airport/ANGB, Minnesota	F-16C (Block 50)	148th FW/OG	ACC	MN
182nd FS (FTU)	JB San Antonio-Kelly Field, Lackland AFB, Texas	F-16C/D (Block 30)	149th FW/OG	AETC	SA
195th FS (FTU)	Tucson International Airport, Arizona	F-16C/D (Block 25/32)	162nd Wing/OG	AETC	AZ
Air Force Reserve Command units					
69th FS (see note 5)	Luke AFB, Arizona	F-16C/D (Block 25/42)	944th FW/OG	AETC	LF
84 TES (see note 6)	Eglin AFB, Florida	F-16C/D (Block 40/50)	926th Wing/OG	ACC	OT
93rd FS	Homestead ARB, Florida	F-16C (Block 30)	482nd FW/OG		FM
457th FS	NAS JRB Fort Worth/Carswell Field, Texas	F-16C/D (Block 30)	301st FW/OG	ACC	TX
466th FS (see note 5)	Hill AFB, Utah	F-16C/D (Block 40)	419th FW/OG		HL
706th FS (see note 6)	Nellis AFB, Nevada	F-16C/D	926th Wing/OG		WA

1	21st FS trains Republic of China Air Force pilots.
2	Active associate unit.
3	425th FS trains Republic of Singapore of Air Force pilots.
4	148th FS trains Royal Netherlands Air Force pilots using Dutch-owned aircraft.
5	AETC gained associate unit operates F-16C/D in support of 56th FW.
6	Classic associate squadron utilizes aircraft assigned to host wing.

ABBREVIATIONS

AACS	Airborne Air Control Squadron	AGRS	Aggressor Squadron	FG	Fighter Group	RAF	Royal Air Force
AAF	Army Air Field	AMARG	Aerospace Maintenance and Regeneration Group	FLTF	Flight Test Flight	RG	Reconnaissance Group
AATC	ANG/AFRC Test Center	AMC	Air Mobility Command	FLTG	Flight Test Group	RQG	Rescue Group
AATTC	Advanced Airlift Tactics Training Center	AMTS	Air Mobility Training Squadron	FLTS	Flight Test Squadron	RQS	Rescue Squadron
AB	Air Base	AMW	Air Mobility Wing	FS	Fighter Squadron	RQW	Rescue Wing
ACA	Aerospace Control Alert	ANG	Air National Guard	FW	Fighter Wing	RS	Reconnaissance Squadron
ACC	Air Combat Command	ANGB	Air National Guard Base	FTG	Flying Training Group	RSO	Remote Split Operations
ACCS	Airborne Command Control Squadron	ANGS	Air National Guard Station	FTOF	Flight Test Operations Facility	RW	Reconnaissance Wing
ACTS	Air Combat Training Squadron	ARB	Air Reserve Base	FTRS	Fighter Training Squadron	SOG	Special Operations Group
ACG	Air Control Group	ARG	Air Refueling Group	FTS	Flying Training Squadron	SOS	Special Operations Squadron
ACW	Air Control Wing	ARS	Air Refueling Squadron	(FTU)	Formal Training Unit	SOW	Special Operations Wing
ADS	Air Demonstration Squadron	ARS	Air Reserve Station	FTW	Flying Training Wing	TEG	Test and Evaluation Group
AETC	Air Education and Training Command	ARW	Air Refueling Wing	HQ	Headquarters	TES	Test and Evaluation Squadron
AFDW	Air Force District of Washington	AS	Airlift Squadron	HG	Helicopter Group	TESTG	Test Group
AFGSC	Air Force Global Strike Command	ASF	Aviation Standards Flight	HS	Helicopter Squadron	TPS	Test Pilot School
AFSAC	Air Force Security Assistance and Cooperation Directorate	ATG	Adversary Tactics Group	IFS	Introductory Flight Screening	TRS	Training Squadron
AFSOAWC	Air Force Special Operations Air Warfare Center	ATKS	Attack Squadron	JARS	Joint Air Reserve Station	TW	Test Wing
AFSOC	Air Force Special Operations Command	ATKW	Attack Wing	JB	Joint Base	USAF	United States Air Force
AFB	Air Force Base	ATRS	Aerial Targets Squadron	JNGS	Joint National Guard Station	USAFA	United States Air Force Academy
AFMC	Air Force Materiel Command	AW	Airlift Wing	JRB	Joint Reserve Base	USAFE	United States Air Forces Europe
AFRC	Air Force Reserve Command	BS	Bomb Squadron	NAF	Naval Air Facility	USAFWC	USAF Weapons Center
AFTC	Air Force Test Center	BW	Bomb Wing	NAS	Naval Air Station	USAFWS	USAF Weapons School
AG	Airlift Group	CACG	Command and Control Group	NSA	Naval Support Activity	USCENTOM	US Central Command
		CCW	Command and Control Wing	OG	Operations Group	USSOUTHCOM	US Southern Command
		CTS	Combat Training Squadron	OS	Operations Squadron	WEG	Weapons Evaluation Group
		Det	Detachment	PACAF	Pacific Air Forces	WPS	Weapons Squadron
		DIA	Defense Intelligence Agency	PAG	Presidential Airlift Group	WRS	Weather Reconnaissance Squadron
		DSCA	Defense Security Co-operation Agency	PAS	Presidential Airlift Squadron		

F-22A Raptor

Considered to be the USAF's premier air dominance fighter, the F-22A was selected as the winner of the Advanced Tactical Fighter (ATF) competition in April 1991. The first of nine engineering and manufacturing development (EMD) aircraft carried out its first flight at the contractor's Marietta, Georgia facility in September 1997.

The 53rd Wing's 422nd Test and Evaluation Squadron at Nellis AFB, Nevada, received the first operational F-22A in July 2003. Deliveries of the type to the 325th Fighter Wing at Tyndall AFB, Florida, began during September 2003.

The first combat-coded Raptors were delivered to the 1st Fighter Wing at Langley AFB, Virginia, in May 2005. The type achieved full operational capability with the wing in December 2007. Lockheed Martin delivered the last of 187 production Raptors to the 3rd Wing at Joint Base Elmendorf-Richardson, Alaska, in May 2012.

Whereas the original increment 1 version was designed as an air superiority fighter, increment 2 added a global strike basic capability, and all operational aircraft were updated to that configuration by 2009. It provided the capability to use AIM-9M and AIM-120C air-to-air missiles and two 1,000lb (454kg) GBU-32 Joint Direct Attack Munitions (JDAMs). The configuration upgraded the intra-flight datalink (IFDL) and provided enhanced connectivity with other Raptors.

Increment 3.1 modifications updated the Northrop Grumman AN/APG-77 radar and provided advanced air-to-ground capabilities that include a synthetic aperture radar (SAR) ground-mapping mode. Improved electronic attack and threat geo-location capabilities allow it to locate enemy radars. The capability to deliver up to eight GBU-39/B Small Diameter Bombs (SDBs) was added.

The increment 3.2A software upgrade afforded additional enhanced electronic protection and improved communications that include a Link 16 datalink receive mode and enhanced combat identification and targeting capabilities. Development testing of the increment 3.2B hardware and software upgrades was completed in April 2017 and initial operational test and evaluation (IOT&E) should be completed by May 2018. Fielding of the first operationally equipped Raptors is set to follow in 2019. It will provide improvements to the IFDL and enhanced stores management system (ESMS). By mid-2020, 152 Raptors will receive the upgrades at a cost of around $1.5 billion. The program will upgrade the F-22's emitter geo-location and electronic protection capabilities and provide AIM-9X Block 2 and AIM-120D integration.

The USAF is moving forward with plans to equip Raptor pilots with a helmet-mounted display system by 2020, along with communications upgrades called TacLink 16 and Tactical Mandates (TACMAN) that will be integrated in 2021 and 2022 respectively.

Once modifications have been completed, the F-22A fleet will comprise 139 combat-coded Block 30/35 jets, 32 training Block 20s, 12 development test/operational test (DT/OT) Block 20/30/35s and two pre-block test aircraft. The Block 30/35 Raptors will include 39 Block 20 aircraft from lots 3 and 4 that will be upgraded.

The service is considering upgrading the 34 remaining Block 20s that support training and test efforts to the combat-coded Block 30/35 configuration, and estimates that such an effort would cost $1.7 billion.

Squadron	Location	Aircraft	Wing/Group	Command	Tail code
19th FS (ASSOC)	JB Pearl Harbor-Hickam, Hawaii	F-22A	15th Wing/OG	PACAF	HH
27th FS	JB Langley-Eustis, Virginia	F-22A	1st FW/OG	ACC	FF
31st TES (see note 1)	Edwards AFB, California	F-22A	53rd Wing/53rd TEG	ACC	ED
43rd FS (FTU)	Tyndall AFB, Florida	F-22A	325th FW/OG	ACC	TY
90th FS	JB Elmendorf-Richardson, Alaska	F-22A	3rd Wing/OG	PACAF	AK
94th FS	JB Langley-Eustis, Virginia	F-22A	1st FW/OG	ACC	TY
95th FS	Tyndall AFB, Florida	F-22A	325th FW/OG	ACC	TY
411th FLTS	Edwards AFB, California	F-22A	412th TW/OG	AFMC	ED
422nd TES	Nellis AFB, Nevada	F-22A	53rd Wing/53rd TEG	ACC	OT
433rd WPS (see note 1)	Nellis AFB, Nevada	F-22A	57th Wing/USAFWS	ACC	WA
525th FS	JB Elmendorf-Richardson, Alaska	F-22A	3rd Wing/OG	PACAF	AK
Air National Guard units					
149th FS (see note 2)	JB Langley-Eustis, Virginia	F-22A	192nd FW/OG	ACC	FF
199th FS	JB Pearl Harbor-Hickam, Hawaii	F-22A	154th Wing/OG	PACAF	HH
Air Force Reserve Command units					
301st FS (see note 2)	Tyndall AFB, Florida	F-22A	301st FW/44th FG	ACC	TY
302nd FS (see note 2)	JB Elmendorf-Richardson, Alaska	F-22A	477th FG	PACAF	AK
706th FS (see note 2)	Nellis AFB, Nevada	F-22A	926th Wing/OG	ACC	WA

1　Squadron utilizes aircraft assigned to host wing.
2　Associate squadron utilizes aircraft assigned to host wing.

An F-22A Raptor from the 1st Fighter Wing deployed to RAF Lakenheath, UK. Jamie Hunter

F-35A Lightning II

The F-35A began its first operational deployment in November 2017 when 12 Lightning IIs operated by the 388th Fighter Wing's 34th Fighter Squadron arrived at Kadena Air Base, Japan. The squadron achieved initial operational capability on August 2, 2016.

The first 10 low-rate initial production (LRIP) lots included more than 175 F-35As and the fighters have now been delivered to five bases. The 33rd Fighter Wing at Eglin AFB, Florida and the 56th Fighter Wing at Luke AFB, Arizona, are responsible for training F-35A pilots. The latter wing trains international Lightning II pilots.

The USAF's plans include the purchase of 1,763 F-35As by 2038. At the end of Fiscal 2017 there were 119 examples of the aircraft in service with ACC, AETC and AFMC. The service plans to field the F-35A to both the Pacific and European theaters in 2020 and 2021. RAF Lakenheath and Eielson AFB, Alaska will both be home to two squadrons of Lightning IIs.

In January 2017, the USAF announced the selection of Naval Air Station Fort Worth Joint Reserve Base, Texas, as the preferred location for the first AFRC-led F-35A unit. The 301st Fighter Wing, which currently operates the F-16C, is expected to receive Lightning IIs during the mid-2020s. The Air Force is evaluating five Air National Guard facilities as part of a plan to determine the next two units that will receive the F-35A. Burlington International Airport, Vermont had previously been named as the first location for an ANG F-35A unit. The 158th Fighter Wing will see the arrival of its first Lightning II in late 2019.

Squadron	Location	Aircraft	Wing/Group	Command	Tail code
4th FS	Hill AFB, Utah	F-35A	388th FW/OG	ACC	HL
6th WPS	Nellis AFB, Nevada	F-35A	57th Wing/USAFWS	ACC	WA
31st TES (see note 1)	Edwards AFB, California	F-35A	53rd Wing/53rd TEG	ACC	OT
34th FS	Hill AFB, Utah	F-35A	388th FW/OG	ACC	HL
58th FS	Eglin AFB, Florida	F-35A	33rd FW/OG	AETC	EG
61st FS	Luke AFB, Arizona	F-35A	56th FW/OG	AETC	LF
62nd FS	Luke AFB, Arizona	F-35A	56th FW/OG	AETC	LF
63rd FS	Luke AFB, Arizona	F-35A	56th FW/OG	AETC	LF
422nd TES	Nellis AFB, Nevada	F-35A	53rd Wing/53rd TEG	ACC	OT
461st FLTS	Edwards AFB, California	F-35A	412th TW/OG	AFMC	ED
Air Force Reserve Command units					
69th FS (see note 2)	Luke AFB, Arizona	F-35A	944th FW/OG	AETC	LF
466th FS (see note 3)	Hill AFB, Utah	F-35A	419th FW/OG	ACC	HI
706th FS (see note 4)	Nellis AFB, Nevada	F-35A	926th Wing/OG	ACC	WA

1 Squadron utilizes aircraft assigned to host wing.
2 AETC-gained associate unit operates F-35A in support of the 56th FW.
3 ACC-gained associate unit operates F-35A alongside the 388th FW.
4 ACC-gained associate unit operates F-35A alongside 422nd TES

F-35As from Hill AFB's 34th FS on deployment to the UK in early 2017. Jamie Hunter

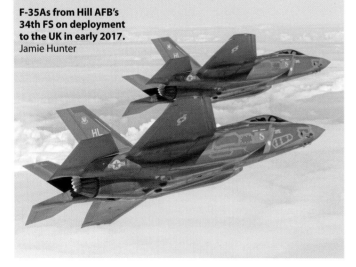

A TH-1H Huey II of the 23rd FTS at Fort Rucker. USAF/MSgt Lance Cheung

UH-1N, TH-1H Iroquois

The USAF has operated a sizeable fleet of UH-1Ns since the first such helicopters entered service in 1970. The initial examples were procured for use in the search and rescue (SAR) role, but today the Twin Hueys are primarily tasked with missile silo, distinguished visitor and survival school support.

The bulk of the UH-1Ns, which are based on the Bell Helicopter Model 212, are operated by AFGSC and the Air Force District of Washington (ADSW). The former's aircraft are tasked with airlifting emergency security and disaster response forces, medical evacuation, security surveillance of off-base movements of nuclear weapons convoys and test range areas, airlift of missile support personnel and airborne cable inspections. The UH-1Ns assigned to the ADSW provide distinguished visitor transport and continuity of government/ continuity of operations (COG/COOP) in the national capital region. The 63 UH-1Ns that are now on the inventory include three examples acquired from the US Marine Corps. The helicopter continues to provide survival school support and conduct SAR missions when required.

The USAF is planning to replace the helicopters with up to 84 in-production, non-developmental, government off-the-shelf or commercial off-the-shelf vertical-lift types. The service released its final request for proposals for the UH-1N replacement program on July 14, 2017. A contract award is expected in spring 2018 and delivery of the first two aircraft will occur no later than 18 months after that.

The USAF also operates 28 TH-1Hs — acquired from the US Army as UH-1Hs — that are operated in the training role at the US Army Aviation Center of Excellence at Cairns Army Airfield, Fort Rucker, Alabama.

Squadron	Location	Aircraft	Wing/Group	Command	Tail code
1st HS	JB Andrews-NAF Washington, Maryland	UH-1N	11th Wing/811th OG	AFDW	
23rd FTS (see note 1)	Lowe AHP, Fort Rucker, Alabama	TH-1H	58th SOW/OG	AETC	FR
36th RQS	Fairchild AFB, Washington	UH-1N	58th SOW/OG	AETC	
37th HS	F. E. Warren AFB, Wyoming	UH-1N	582nd HG	AFGSC	FE
40th HS	Malmstrom AFB, Montana	UH-1N	582nd HG	AFGSC	MM
54th HS	Minot AFB, North Dakota	UH-1N	582nd HG	AFGSC	MT
413th FLTS	Duke Field, Florida	UH-1N	96th TW/OG	AFMC	ET
459th AS	Yokota AB, Japan	UH-1N	374th AW/OG	PACAF	YJ
512th RQS	Kirtland AFB, New Mexico	UH-1N	58th SOW/OG	AETC	
Air National Guard units					
188th RQS (see note 2)	Kirtland AFB, New Mexico	UH-1N	150th SOW/OG	AETC	

1 Crews perform rotary-wing qualification course (RWQC) and specialized undergraduate pilot training — helicopter (SUPT-H).
2 Associate unit conducts training alongside the active-duty 512th SOS.

HH-60G Pave Hawk

The Sikorsky HH-60G is tasked with recovering isolated personnel from hostile or denied territory. When required, it can also conduct humanitarian missions, civil search and rescue, disaster relief, casualty and medical evacuation, and non-combatant evacuation operations. Originally developed from the US Army's UH-60A utility helicopter, the Pave Hawk entered service in a special operations configuration under the designation MH-60G and achieved initial operational capability (IOC) in 1982.

The HH-60G configuration features an external refueling boom and probe that allow the Pave Hawk to refuel from HC/ KC/MC-130 tankers. The cockpit is compatible with night vision goggles, and equipped with a low-altitude warning system and satellite communications (SATCOM). Its mission equipment includes color weather radar, an electro-optical/infra-red (EO/IR) sensor, radar warning receiver, chaff/flare dispensers, infra-red jamming system, hover infra-red suppression system (HIRSS), defensive weapons and a hydraulic rescue hoist. Since entering service attrition has reduced the fleet, which originally included 112 HH-60Gs, to just 97 airframes.

Procurement of up to 24 UH-60Ms had originally been planned as part of the HH-60 operational loss replacement (OLR) mission modification program. The service acquired three UH-60Ms that were modified to rescue configuration by the Army Aviation and Missile Research Development and Engineering Center (AMRDEC) at Redstone Arsenal, Alabama. The first HH-60U was delivered in September 2011 and the three aircraft were subsequently assigned to a 'non-deploying test unit.' Although a number of UH-60Ms were funded, the service transferred them to the Army in exchange for 21 'low-time' UH-60Ls.

The UH-60Ls are being modified to the present-day Air Force HH-60G configuration. As indicated by its name, the program is intended to replace aircraft that have been written off and return the fleet to its original size.

The conversions are being carried out by Science and Engineering Services Inc (SES), which unveiled the first 'new' HH-60G during a ceremony at its Huntsville facility, near the US Army's Redstone Arsenal in Alabama, on June 28, 2016. The initial OLR HH-60G was subsequently delivered to Nellis AFB, Nevada, where it is undergoing developmental testing. Production OLR conversions began in September when the first UH-60L arrived at the SES facility from Davis-Monthan AFB, Arizona.

Squadron	Location	Aircraft	Wing/Group	Command	Tail code
Det 3, AFTC	Nellis AFB, Nevada	HH-60U	AFMC/AFTC	AFMC	
33rd RQS	Kadena AB, Okinawa	HH-60G	18th Wing/OG	PACAF	ZZ
Det 1, 33rd RQS	Osan AB, Republic of Korea	HH-60G	18th Wing/OG	PACAF	ZZ
34th WPS	Nellis AFB, Nevada	HH-60G	57th Wing/USAFWS	ACC	WA
41st RQS	Moody AFB, Georgia	HH-60G	23rd Wing/347th RQG	ACC	FT
55th RQS	Davis-Monthan AFB, Arizona	HH-60G	23rd Wing/563rd RQG	ACC	FT
56th RQS (see note 1)	RAF Lakenheath, Suffolk, England	HH-60G	48th FW/OG	USAFE	LN
66th RQS	Nellis AFB, Nevada	HH-60G	23rd Wing/563rd RQG	ACC	FT
88th TES (see note 2)	Nellis AFB, Nevada	HH-60G	53rd Wing/TEG	ACC	OT
Det 1, 413th FLTS (see note 3)	Nellis AFB, Nevada	HH-60G	96th TW/OG	AFMC	
512th RQS	Kirtland AFB, New Mexico	HH-60G	58th SOW/OG	AETC	
Air National Guard units					
101st RQS	Francis S. Gabreski Airport/ANGB, Westhampton Beach, New York	HH-60G	106th RQW/OG	ACC	
129th RQS	Moffett Federal Airport ANGS, California	HH-60G	129th RQW/OG	ACC	CA
188th RQS (see note 4)	Kirtland AFB, New Mexico	HH-60G	150th SOW/OG	AETC	
210th RQS	JB Elmendorf-Richardson, Alaska	HH-60G	176th Wing/OG	PACAF	
Det 1, 210th RQS	Eielson AFB, Alaska	HH-60G	176th Wing/OG	PACAF	
Air Force Reserve Command units					
301st RQS	Patrick AFB, Florida	HH-60G	920th RQW/OG	ACC	FL
305th RQS	Davis-Monthan AFB, Arizona	HH-60G	920th RQW/943rd RQG	ACC	DR

1   56th RQS will relocate to Aviano AB, Italy, along with the 57th RQS by June 2018.
2   Squadron utilizes aircraft assigned to host wing. Combat Search and Rescue Combined Task Force (CSAR/CTF).
3   Det 1, 413th FLTS is part of the Combat Search and Rescue Combined Test Force.
4   Associate unit conducts training alongside the active-duty 512th SOS.

Contracts are in place for the remaining 20 aircraft and deliveries will be completed by June 2019. Plans call for 18 of the OLR HH-60Gs to be allocated to three ANG rescue squadrons, with the final three being assigned to units at Nellis.

In June 2014, the USAF awarded Sikorsky Aircraft and Lockheed Martin a $1.2-billion contract to develop a new combat rescue helicopter based on the US Army's UH-60M variant. The service plans to acquire 112 HH-60Ws at a cost of $9 billion. Four engineering development model (EDM) aircraft were included in the initial contract. The first HH-60W will fly in 2019 and IOC is planned for 2021.

The USAF subsequently exercised a $203-million contract option with Sikorsky Aircraft for five system demonstration test article (SDTA) HH-60Ws, which will support operational test and training. Sikorsky recently began major assembly of the first HH-60W at its production facility in Bridgeport, Connecticut. It is expected to fly by 2019. Deliveries to the USAF will start in early 2019 and run through 2020, in support of initial operational test and evaluation. Plans call for the USAF to order 18 further aircraft under two low-rate initial production (LRIP) batches in 2019 and 2021. The first combat-coded aircraft will be delivered to Moody AFB, Georgia, and training operations will begin at Kirtland AFB, New Mexico.

A pararescueman, assigned to the 56th Rescue Squadron, rappels from an HH-60G Pave Hawk at RAF Lakenheath, UK. USAF/SSgt Trevor T. McBride

An MQ-9 Reaper operated by the New York Air National Guard's 174th Attack Wing. USAF/MSgt Eric Miller

MQ-1B Predator, MQ-9 Reaper

Produced by General Atomics Aeronautical Systems, the MQ-1B Predator is an armed, multi-mission, Tier II medium-altitude, long-endurance (MALE) remotely piloted aircraft (RPA). The Predator A flew for the first time in July 1994. While still under development, the intelligence, surveillance and reconnaissance (ISR) platform was deployed to Bosnia in July 1995. A more capable Block I RQ-1B version that featured numerous upgrades including a more powerful, turbocharged 105hp (78.3kW) Rotax 914 UL piston engine and de-icing equipment was first deployed in April 2001. The MQ-1B, which was first fielded in 2002, featured a strike capability that included two laser-guided AGM-114 Hellfire air-to-ground missiles. Predator A production for the USAF ended when the final air vehicle was delivered in March 2011.

The RPA's ISR system includes the AN/AAS-52 multi-spectral targeting system (MTS-A), which integrates an infra-red sensor, color/monochrome daylight TV

camera, image-intensified TV camera, laser designator and illuminator. Full-motion video from each of the imaging sensors can be viewed as separate video streams or fused together.

Predators have operated from numerous forward bases, and carried out combat missions over Afghanistan, Bosnia, Serbia, Iraq, Yemen, Libya, Syria, and Somalia. Operations in Afghanistan came to a close in July 2017, when the 361st Expeditionary Attack Squadron carried out its final flight with the MQ-1B. Air Force Special Operations Command had retired its last Predators in February 2016.

The Predators are deployed as systems, each consisting of four air vehicles, a ground control station (GCS), launch and recovery element (LRE) and a satellite communication suite that allows the mission control element (MCE) to be located thousands of miles away from the operating base. Although it is operated by active-duty, ANG and AFRC reconnaissance units, phase-out of the MQ-1B is under way. According to ACC, the last Predators are scheduled for retirement by spring 2018 depending on mission requirements.

Development of a 'growth version' of the MQ-1 began as a company-funded project during 1999. General Atomics conducted the first flight of its Predator B at the company's flight operations facility in El Mirage, California during February 2001. Known as the Reaper, the MQ-9A is powered by a single Honeywell TPE-331 turboprop engine that permits it to fly at altitudes up to 50,000ft (15,240m). It can operate at greater stand-off ranges for up to 12 hours, and its larger internal payload allows it to simultaneously carry multiple sensors weighting up to 800lb (363kg).

The Reaper shares a common avionics system with the MQ-1B and interfaces with the same ground control station but is equipped with triple-redundant avionics and dual mechanical control systems that meet the requirements for flight in the US national air space (NAS).

The MQ-9A was first fielded operationally in March 2007 and deployed to Afghanistan in September 2007. It carried out its inaugural combat strike in late October. General Atomics delivered the last of 195 Block 1 MQ-9As to the Air Force in mid-2015 and transitioned production to the Block 5 variant. Its features include improved main landing gear, an upgraded electrical system, additional radio, encrypted datalinks, a redesigned avionics bay and digital electronic engine control system, the BRU-71 bomb rack and HD video. The USAF's acquisition plans include 155 Block 5 RPAs. It will upgrade its surviving Block 1 variants.

The Block 5 version first saw combat on June 23, 2017, when and RPA delivered a GBU-38 JDAM and two Hellfire missiles against IS targets. More than 250 Reapers are in service with active-duty, ANG and AFRC squadrons. In addition to converting the remaining Predator squadrons to the MQ-9A, the USAF is planning further expansion and will be establishing more Reaper units. Shaw AFB, South Carolina, had been named as the preferred location for a Reaper group that will be activated in 2018. Although the new group will include mission control elements (MCE), Reapers will not be stationed at or flown from Shaw. The Air Force is still considering locations that will host a complete Reaper wing that will include as many as 24 MQ-9s, launch and recovery elements (LREs), an MCE, a maintenance group and support personnel. Shaw remains under consideration for that mission along with Eglin AFB and Tyndall AFB in Florida and Vandenberg AFB, California.

The MQ-9A's systems include an AN/APY-8 Lynx II radar that features synthetic aperture radar (SAR), ground/dismount moving target indicator (GMTI/DMTI) modes and the AN/AAS-52 MTS-B, which integrates an infra-red sensor, color/monochrome daylight TV camera, image-intensified TV camera, laser rangefinder/designator, and laser illuminator. The 'hunter-killer' is equipped with four wing hardpoints that allow the Reaper to carry up to 3,000lb (1,361kg) of weapons. Its stores include up to eight laser-guided AGM-114 missiles and other munitions such as the GBU-12 Paveway II laser-guided bomb and GBU-38 Joint Direct Attack Munitions.

The USAF began fielding the extended-range (ER) version of the Reaper, which boosts its endurance from 27 to 33-35 hours, during 2015. Developed as a quick reaction capability (QRC), the modifications equip the Reaper with new wings containing extra fuel tanks and winglets, the capability to carry external fuel tanks, a four-blade propeller, anti-

Squadron	Location	Aircraft	Wing/Group	Command	Tail code
15th ATKS	Creech AFB, Nevada	MQ-1B	432nd Wing/OG	ACC	CH
Det 1, 31st TES	Grey Butte FTOF, Palmdale, California	MQ-1B	53rd Wing/TEG	ACC	CH
Det 1, 452nd FLTS	Grey Butte FTOF, Palmdale, California	MQ-1B	412th TW/OG	AFMC	
556th TES (see note 1)	Creech AFB, Nevada	MQ-1B	53rd Wing/TEG	ACC	CH
558th FTS (see note 2)	JB San Antonio-Randolph, Texas	MQ-1B	12th FTW/OG	AETC	RA
Air National Guard units					
162nd RS	Springfield-Beckley Municipal Airport, Ohio	MQ-1B RSO	178th Wing/OG	ACC	

1   Squadron utilizes aircraft assigned to host wing.
2   558th FTS conducts undergraduate remotely piloted aircraft training.

Squadron	Location	Aircraft	Wing/Group	Command	Tail code
3rd SOS	Cannon AFB, New Mexico	MQ-9A	27th SOW/OG	AFSOC	
6th ATKS (FTU)	Holloman AFB, New Mexico	MQ-9A	49th Wing/OG	ACC	HO
9th ATKS (FTU)	Holloman AFB, New Mexico	MQ-9A	49th Wing/OG	ACC	HO
11th ATKS (FTU)	Creech AFB, Nevada	MQ-9A	432nd Wing/OG	ACC	CH
12th SOS (see note 1)	Cannon AFB, New Mexico	MQ-9A	27th SOW/OG	AFSOC	
15th ATKS	Creech AFB, Nevada	MQ-9A	432nd Wing/OG	ACC	CH
17th ATKS	Creech AFB, Nevada	MQ-9A	432nd Wing/732nd OG	ACC	CH
20th ATKS	Creech AFB, Nevada	MQ-9A	432nd Wing/OG	ACC	CH
22nd ATKS	Creech AFB, Nevada	MQ-9A	432nd Wing/732nd OG	ACC	CH
29th ATKS (FTU)	Holloman AFB, New Mexico	MQ-9A	49th Wing/OG	ACC	HO
26th WPS (see note 2)	Creech AFB, Nevada	MQ-9A	57th Wing/USAFWS	ACC	CH
30th RS	Tonopah Test Range, Nevada	MQ-9A	432nd Wing/732nd OG	ACC	
Det 1, 31st TES	Grey Butte FTOF, Palmdale, California	MQ-9A	53rd Wing/TEG	ACC	
33rd SOS	Cannon AFB, New Mexico	MQ-9A	27th SOW/OG	AFSOC	
42nd ATKS	Creech AFB, Nevada	MQ-9A	432nd Wing/OG	ACC	CH
89th ATKS	Ellsworth AFB, South Dakota	MQ-9A RSO	432nd Wing/OG	ACC	
Det 1, 452nd FLTS	Grey Butte FTOF, Palmdale, California	MQ-9A	412th TW/OG	AFMC	
489th ATKS	Creech AFB, Nevada	MQ-9A	432nd Wing/OG	ACC	CH
556th TES (see note 2)	Creech AFB, Nevada	MQ-9A	53rd Wing/TEG	ACC	CH
867th ATKS	Creech AFB, Nevada	MQ-9A	432nd Wing/OG	ACC	CH
Air National Guard units					
103rd ATKS	Horsham AGS, Pennsylvania	MQ-9A RSO	111th ATKW/OG	ACC	
105th ATKS	Nashville International Airport-JB Berry Field, Tennessee	MQ-9A RSO	118th Wing/OG	ACC	
108th ATKS (FTU)	Syracuse Hancock International Airport, New York	MQ-9A	174th ATKW/OG	ACC	
111th ATKS	Ellington Field JRB, Houston, Texas	MQ-9A	147th ATKW/OG	ACC	EL
124th ATKS	Des Moines International Airport, Iowa	MQ-9A RSO	132nd Wing/OG	ACC	
136th ATKS	Niagara Falls International Airport/JARS, New York	MQ-9A RSO	107th ATKW/OG	ACC	
138th ATKS	Syracuse Hancock International Airport, New York	MQ-9A	174th ATKW/OG	ACC	
172nd ATKS	W. K. Kellogg Regional Airport/ANGB, Battle Creek, Michigan	MQ-9A RSO	110th ATKW/OG	ACC	
178th ATKS	Hector International Airport, Fargo, North Dakota	MQ-9A	119th Wing/OG	ACC	
184th ATKS	Fort Smith Regional Airport/Ebbing ANGB, Arkansas	MQ-9A RSO	188th Wing/OG	ACC	
196th ATKS	March ARB, California	MQ-9A	163rd ATKW/OG	ACC	
214th ATKS	Davis-Monthan AFB, Arizona	MQ-1B	162nd Wing/214th ATKG	ACC	AZ
232nd OS (see note 3)	Creech AFB, Nevada	MQ-9A	152nd AW/OG	ACC	CH
Air Force Reserve Command units					
2nd SOS	Hurlburt Field, Florida	MQ-9A RSO	919th SOW/SOG	AFSOC	
78th ATKS (see note 4)	Creech AFB, Nevada	MQ-9A	926th Wing/726th OG	ACC	CH
91st ATKS (see note 3)	Creech AFB, Nevada	MQ-9A	926th Wing/726th OG	ACC	CH
429th ACTS (see note 5)	Holloman AFB, New Mexico	MQ-9A	926th Wing/726th OG	ACC	HO

1 LRE operations.
2 Squadron utilizes aircraft assigned to host wing.
3 Associate squadron integrated integrated with the USAF AWC and the 432nd Wing. Primarily supports 556th TES MQ-9A operational test and evaluation mission.
4 78th ATKS and 91st ATKS are associate units and are integrated with the 432nd Wing.
5 429th ACTS operates MQ-9s assigned to the 49th Wing.

Squadron	Location	Aircraft	Wing/Group	Command	Tail code
Det 4, 9th OG	NAS Sigonella, Italy	RQ-4B	9th RW/OG	ACC	BB
Det 2, 53rd TEG (see note 1)	Beale AFB, California	RQ-4B	53rd Wing	ACC	BB
Det 1, 69th RG	Andersen AFB, Guam	RQ-4B (Block 40)	9th RW/69th RG	ACC	GF
1st RS (FTU)	Beale AFB, California	RQ-4B (Block 30)	9th RW/OG	ACC	BB
12th RS	Beale AFB, California	RQ-4B (Block 30)	9th RW/OG	ACC	BB
348th RS	Grand Forks AFB, North Dakota	EQ-4B, RQ-4B (Block 40)	9th RW/69th RG	ACC	GF
31st TES (see note 1)	Edwards AFB, California	RQ-4B	53rd Wing	ACC	ED
452nd FLTS	Edwards AFB, California	RQ-4B	412th TW/OG	AFMC	ED
Air Force Reserve Command units					
13th RS (see note 2)	Beale AFB, California	RQ-4B	926th Wing/726th OG	ACC	BB

1 Squadron utilizes aircraft assigned to host wing.
2 13th RS is an associate unit and is integrated with the 9th RW.

RQ-4B Global Hawk

First flown in February 1998, the Global Hawk was developed by Teledyne Ryan Aeronautical, which is now part of Northrop Grumman. Assigned the designation RQ-4A, it was one of two high-altitude, long-endurance remotely-piloted aircraft (RPA) originally developed for the Tier 2+ unmanned air system (UAS) program. Seven development aircraft were followed by seven Block 10 production RQ-4As. The surviving RQ-4As were retired in 2011 and were transferred to the US Navy and to NASA.

First flown in March 2007, the Block 20 RQ-4B retained the A-model's integrated sensor suite (ISS) that included an electro-optical (EO), infra-red (IR), synthetic aperture radar (SAR) payload and limited signals intelligence (SIGINT)-gathering capability. It featured numerous improvements to the structure and powerplant, and its payload was doubled.

The first of six Block 20s entered service in June 2008. Two examples were written off and the others were converted to EQ-4B communication relay configuration, carrying the Battlefield Airborne Communication Node (BACN) payload.

The Block 30 RQ-4B is a multi-intelligence platform that simultaneously carries EO, IR, SAR, and high- and low-band SIGINT sensors. It first flew at Air Force Plant 42 in Palmdale, California, in November 2007, and achieved initial operating capability (IOC) in August 2011. Through October 2017, Northrop Grumman had delivered 18 Block 30s.

The first of 11 Block 40 RQ-4Bs was unveiled at Plant 42 in June 2009. It features the Northrop Grumman AN/ZPY-2 multi-platform radar technology insertion program (RTIP) active electronically scanned array radar.

The Block 40 RQ-4B made its combat debut in September 2013 and achieved IOC that October.

ACC now operates four EQ-4Bs and 27 RQ-4Bs, including two of the latter that are assigned to the AFMC. Each RQ-4B system is comprised of two air vehicles, a launch and recovery element (LRE) and a mission control element (MCE). To date, the USAF has procured nine MCEs and 10 LREs.

Development of additional systems for the RQ-4B continues and Northrop Grumman carried out tests with an UTC Aerospace Systems MS-177 multi-spectral sensor in February 2017.

Airmen with the 69th Reconnaissance Group, Detachment 1, prepare an RQ-4 Global Hawk for a mission from Yokota Air Base, Japan.
USAF/A1C Donald Hudson

ice/de-ice system and a new fuel management system.

First flown in February 2014, initial flight-testing of the variant ended that June. The USAF procured 38 modification kits in response to a joint urgent operational needs statement (JUONS). The newest version was operationally fielded in 2015 by AFSOC. ACC completed operational testing in September 2015 and approved fielding in November 2015. The service plans to convert its Block 5 Reapers to ER configuration under its follow-on Reaper capability enhancement (FORCE) project. As of September 30, 2017, there were 121 MQ-1Bs and 218 MQ-9As in service with ACC, AFMC, AFSOC and the ANG.

RQ-170A Sentinel

The RQ-170A is a low-observable unmanned aircraft system (UAS) that was first sighted around Kandahar Airfield, Afghanistan, in 2007. Although the program officially remains classified even now, some 10 years later, the USAF confirmed the existence of the flying-wing Sentinel in December 2009.

Developed by Lockheed Martin's Skunk Works, the single-engine intelligence, surveillance and reconnaissance air systems are operated by ACC's 432nd Wing from Creech AFB and the Tonopah Test Range in Nevada.

Squadron	Location	Aircraft	Wing/Group	Command	Tail code
30th RS	Tonopah Test Range, Nevada	RQ-170A	432nd Wing/732nd OG	ACC	
44th RS	Creech AFB, Nevada	RQ-170A	432nd Wing/732nd OG	ACC	

A T-1A Jayhawk of the 99th Flying Training Squadron, 12th Flying Training Wing, Randolph AFB. USAF/Greg L. Davis

Squadron	Location	Aircraft	Wing/Group	Command	Tail code
3rd FTS	Vance AFB, Oklahoma	T-1A	71st FTW/OG	AETC	VN
48th FTS	Columbus AFB, Mississippi	T-1A	14th FTW/OG	AETC	CB
86th FTS	Laughlin AFB, Texas	T-1A	47th FTW/OG	AETC	XL
99th FTS	JB San Antonio-Randolph, Texas	T-1A	12th FTW/OG	AETC	RA
451st FTS	NAS Pensacola, Florida	T-1A	12th FTW/479th FTG	AETC	AP
Air Force Reserve Command units					
5th FTS (see note 1)	Vance AFB, Oklahoma	T-1A	340th FTG	AETC	VN
39th FTS (see note 1)	JB San Antonio-Randolph, Texas	T-1A	340th FTG	AETC	RA
43rd FTS (see note 1)	Columbus AFB, Mississippi	T-1A	340th FTG	AETC	CB
96th FTS (see note 1)	Laughlin AFB, Texas	T-1A	340th FTG	AETC	XL

1   AETC-gained associate unit that provides instructor pilots for T-1A and utilizes aircraft assigned to host wing.

T-1A Jayhawk

The Beechjet 400T was selected as the winner of a USAF competition for a Tanker/Transport Training System (TTTS) in February 1990. It was based on the Mitsubishi MU-300 Diamond. Deliveries to Reese AFB, Texas began in January 1992 and student training commenced in 1993. Today the Jayhawk supports the advanced phase of specialized undergraduate pilot training (SUPT) and the advanced phase of undergraduate combat systems officer (CSO) training (UCT). The T-1A provides cockpit seating for an instructor and two students and four passenger seats are installed in the cabin.

The 21 Jayhawks used for CSO training have been upgraded with a suite of simulated sensors, countermeasures and weapon systems as well as provision for two students and two instructors. Deliveries of the modified T-1As began in mid-2011 and were completed in August 2012. A follow-on upgrade that allowed the aircraft to be used for airborne electronic warfare training was competed in January 2014.

The USAF acquired 180 T-1As and 178 remain on the inventory. A planned T-1A avionics modernization program will allow the Jayhawk fleet to remain in service until the 2050 timeframe.

T-6A Texan II

The USAF operates a fleet of 444 T-6As, which serve as primary trainers at five AETC bases and one naval air station. The Texan II was initially known as the Beech MkII and was developed from the Pilatus PC-9. It was selected to replace the USAF's T-37B and the US Navy's T-34C trainers as the winner of the Joint Primary Aircraft Training System (JPATS) competition in June 1995. It flew for the first time at Beech Field, Wichita, Kansas, in July 1998 and achieved Initial operational capability (IOC) in July 2002. The USAF accepted the last of 454 T-6As from Beechcraft in May 2010. The aircraft, which is powered by a single Pratt & Whitney Canada PT6-68D turboprop, also support the primary phase of the undergraduate combat systems officer (CSO) training program. Texan IIs are assigned to 10 active-duty flying training squadrons. Training efforts are supported by five AFRC associate squadrons at five primary training bases.

An L3 Communications crew chief marshals a T-6 Texan II at Vance AFB, Oklahoma. USAF/David Poe

Squadron	Location	Aircraft	Wing/Group	Command	Tail code
8th FTS	Vance AFB, Oklahoma	T-6A	71st FTW/OG	AETC	VN
33rd FTS	Vance AFB, Oklahoma	T-6A	71st FTW/OG	AETC	VN
37th FTS	Columbus AFB, Mississippi	T-6A	14th FTW/OG	AETC	CB
41st FTS	Columbus AFB, Mississippi	T-6A	14th FTW/OG	AETC	CB
85th FTS	Laughlin AFB, Texas	T-6A	47th FTW/OG	AETC	XL
89th FTS	Sheppard AFB, Texas	T-6A	80th FTW/OG	AETC	EN
434th FTS	Laughlin AFB, Texas	T-6A	47th FTW/OG	AETC	XL
455th FTS	NAS Pensacola, Florida	T-6A	12th FTW/479th FTG	AETC	AP
459th FTS	Sheppard AFB, Texas	T-6A	80th FTW/OG	AETC	EN
559th FTS	JB San Antonio-Randolph, Texas	T-6A	12th FTW/OG	AETC	RA
Air Force Reserve Command units					
5th FTS (see note 1)	Vance AFB, Oklahoma	T-6A	340th FTG	AETC	VN
39th FTS (see note 1)	JB San Antonio-Randolph, Texas	T-6A	340th FTG	AETC	RA
43rd FTS (see note 1)	Columbus AFB, Mississippi	T-6A	340th FTG	AETC	CB
96th FTS (see note 1)	Laughlin AFB, Texas	T-6A	340th FTG	AETC	XL
97th FTS (see note 1)	Sheppard AFB, Texas	T-6A	340th FTG	AETC	EN

1   AETC-gained associate unit, provides instructor pilots for T-6A and utilizes aircraft assigned to host wing.

MISCELLANEOUS TYPES

UV-18B Twin Otter
Three UV-18Bs support the US Air Force Academy (USAFA).

USAFA gliders
The USAFA's soaring program utilizes several types of sailplanes.

T-41D Mescalero
The USAFA operates four T-41Ds for basic airmanship.

T-51A
Three Cessna Model 150s are used by the USAFA Flying Team.

T-53A Kaydet II
The 557th Flying Training Squadron operates 24 Cirrus SR20s for airmanship training.

DA20-C1
A fleet of Diamond Aircraft DA20-C1 trainers supports the USAF's initial flight training (IFT) program.

Full details of these types and their units appeared in the 2017 edition of the *United States Air Force Air Power Yearbook*.

Squadron	Location	Aircraft	Wing/Group	Command	Tail code
1st RS (FTU)	Beale AFB, California	T-38A	9th RW/OG	ACC	BB
2nd FTRS	Tyndall AFB, Florida	T-38A/B/C	325th FW/OG	ACC	TY
25th FTS	Vance AFB, Oklahoma	T-38C	71st FTW/OG	AETC	VN
49th FTRS	Columbus AFB, Mississippi	AT-38C	14th FTW/OG	AETC	CB
50th FTS	Columbus AFB, Mississippi	T-38C	14th FTW/OG	AETC	CB
71st FTRS	JB Langley-Eustis, Virginia	T-38A/B	1st FW/OG	ACC	FF
87th FTS	Laughlin AFB, Texas	T-38C	47th FTW/OG	AETC	XL
88th FTRS	Sheppard AFB, Texas	AT-38C	80th FTW/OG	AETC	EN
90th FTS	Sheppard AFB, Texas	T-38C	80th FTW/OG	AETC	EN
99th RS	Beale AFB, California	T-38A	9th RW/OG	ACC	BB
394th CTS (FTU)	Whiteman AFB, Missouri	T-38A	509th BW/OG	AFGSC	WM
416th FLTS	Edwards AFB, California	T-38C	412th TW/OG	AFMC	ED
435th FTRS	JB San Antonio-Randolph, Texas	AT-38C	12th FTW/OG	AETC	RA
469th FTS	Sheppard AFB, Texas	T-38C	80th FTW/OG	AETC	EN
560th FTS	JB San Antonio-Randolph, Texas	T-38C	12th FTW/OG	AETC	RA
586th FLTS	Holloman AFB, New Mexico	T-38C	AEDC/704th TESTG	AFMC	HT
Air Force Reserve Command units					
5th FTS (see note 1)	Vance AFB, Oklahoma	T-38C	340th FTG	AETC	VN
39th FTS (see note 1)	JB San Antonio-Randolph, Texas	T-38C, AT-38C	340th FTG	AETC	RA
43rd FTS (see note 1)	Columbus AFB, Mississippi	T-38C, AT-38C	340th FTG	AETC	CB
96th FTS (see note 1)	Laughlin AFB, Texas	T-38C	340th FTG	AETC	XL
97th FTS (see note 1)	Sheppard AFB, Texas	T-38C, AT-38C	340th FTG	AETC	EN

1   AETC-gained associate unit, provides instructor pilots for T/AT-38C and utilizes aircraft assigned to host wing.

T-38A/B/C, AT-38C Talon

The Talon has been the USAF's advanced trainer since the first T-38As entered service in March 1961. It is powered by two General Electric J85-GE-5 turbojet engines and is capable of high-altitude, supersonic flight. Between 1961 and 1972 more than 1,100 Talons were delivered to the USAF and 503 are now in service with AETC, ACC, AFGSC and AFMC units.

In support of the advanced phase of the USAF's specialized undergraduate pilot training (SUPT) program, 429 T-38Cs provide students with advanced flying training. Talons are used as lead-in fighter trainers, under the introduction to fighter fundamentals (IFF) program, and perform pilot instructor training (PIT) and Euro-NATO Joint Jet Pilot Training (ENJJPT) undergraduate pilot training (UPT). A further 15 examples assigned to AFMC

support the USAF Test Pilot School and test and evaluation efforts.

Although they were retired from the UPT role in May 2007, 47 T-38As and six T-38Bs continue to serve as companion trainers and as aggressor aircraft in support of the U-2S, B-2A and F-22A fleets.

Between 2001 and 2007, 463 T-38As and AT-38Bs were equipped with digital 'glass' cockpits under the avionics upgrade program (AUP). The aircraft also underwent a propulsion modernization program (PMP). Under the Pacer Classic effort, Boeing is ensuring the airworthiness of 150 T-38s through a series of structural modifications. Pacer Classic III will maintain the T-38 fleet's viability until 2029.

The USAF formally launched its T-X trainer competition on December 30, 2016 when it released the final request for proposals for the Advanced Pilot Training (APT) project, which will ultimately replace the T-38C.

A T-38A Talon of the 2nd Fighter Training Squadron at Tyndall AFB. USAF/MSgt Burt Traynor

A U-2S flies over the Golden Gate Bridge near San Francisco, California. USAF/SSgt Robert M. Trujillo

U-2S/TU-2S 'Dragon Lady'

Although the initial Lockheed U-2A first flew in August 1955, today's U-2S is a significantly larger and more capable platform than the original high-altitude reconnaissance aircraft. Known unofficially as the 'Dragon Lady', the aircraft is the USAF's sole manned strategic reconnaissance asset.

Lockheed delivered 12 U-2Rs between 1967 and 1970; 18 similar TR-1As followed from 1981 to 1993. Although the TR-1A was a tactical reconnaissance version it was structurally identical to the U-2R.

In 1991 the aircraft were all redesignated as U-2Rs. Beginning in 1994 they were upgraded with a single General Electric F118-GE-101 turbofan engine, and after receiving this modification they received the designation U-2S. The two-seat training variant is called the TU-2S.

The U-2S can be equipped with multiple sensors including cameras, infra-red and radar systems, electronic intelligence packages and the Advanced

Synthetic Aperture Radar System 2A (ASARS-2A). Another major system is the Senior Year electro-optical reconnaissance system-2C (SYERS 2C).

Plans to retain the U-2S and retire the Global Hawk were reversed in 2015 and the 'Dragon Lady's' phase-out was scheduled to begin during 2019. In May 2017, the service backed away from those plans and it will now retain the U-2 fleet indefinitely.

As a result of that decision, the U-2S will likely field the more advanced ASARS-2B sensor package, which will feature an active electronically scanned array (AESA) radar and other new capabilities. The radar is presently under development by Raytheon.

ACC's fleet today includes 27 U-2S and four TU-2S models that are assigned to the 9th Reconnaissance Wing at Beale AFB, California. The aircraft are also permanently deployed to Osan AB, South Korea, under the 5th Reconnaissance Squadron and to RAF Akrotiri, Cyprus, under the 9th OG Det 1, as well as carrying out temporary deployments to Europe and South-west Asia.

Squadron	Location	Aircraft	Wing/Group	Command	Tail code
Det 1, 9th OG	RAF Akrotiri, Cyprus	U-2S	9th RW/OG	ACC	BB
Det 2, 53rd TEG (see note 1)	Beale AFB, California	U-2S	53rd Wing/OG	ACC	BB
1st RS (FTU)	Beale AFB, California	U-2S, TU-2S	9th RW/OG	ACC	BB
5th RS	Osan AB, Republic of Korea	U-2S	9th RW/OG	ACC	BB
99th RS	Beale AFB, California	U-2S	9th RW/OG	ACC	BB

1   Squadron utilizes aircraft assigned to host wing.

U-28A

Based on the single-engine Pilatus PC-12/45 light transport, the U-28A provides tactical airborne intelligence, surveillance, reconnaissance (AISR) and targeting in support of theater special operations forces (SOF). An initial batch of six PC-12s was purchased by US Special Operations Command from commercial sources in 2005 and modified for use in support of Operations 'Enduring Freedom' and 'Iraqi Freedom'.

Modifications that were carried out by the Sierra Nevada Corporation (SNC) at its facility in Hagerstown, Maryland equipped the aircraft with military-specific communications and aircraft survivability equipment (ASE), electro-optical/infra-red (EO/IR) sensors, and advanced navigation systems equipment. Its advanced communications suite includes datalinks that can transmit high-definition full-motion video (FMV), data, and voice communications. Upgrades have provided the aircraft with high-definition (HD), FMV and signals intelligence (SIGINT) capability. The fleet recently received improved GPS kit and upgraded infra-red suppression equipment as well as enhanced multi-spectral

Squadron	Location	Aircraft	Wing/Group	Command	Tail code
14th WPS (see note 1)	Hurlburt Field, Florida	U-28A	57th Wing/USAFWS	ACC	
19th SOS (FTU) (see note 1)	Hurlburt Field, Florida	U-28A	492nd SOW/SOG	AFSOC	
34th SOS	Hurlburt Field, Florida	U-28A	1st SOW/SOG	AFSOC	
318th SOS	Cannon AFB, New Mexico	U-28A	27th SOW/SOG	AFSOC	
319th SOS	Hurlburt Field, Florida	U-28A	1st SOW/SOG	AFSOC	
551st SOS (FTU) (see note 1)	Cannon AFB, New Mexico	U-28A	492nd SOW/SOG	AFSOC	
Air Force Reserve Command units					
5th SOS (see note 2)	Hurlburt Field, Florida	U-28A	919th SOW/SOG	AFSOC	

1   Utilizes aircraft assigned to host wing.
2   Associate squadron utilizes aircraft assigned to host wing.

targeting system (MTS-B) sensors. The U-28A forms part of AFSOC's light tactical fixed-wing fleet, which was previously known as non-standard aviation. The 28-aircraft fleet is operated by five special operations squadrons stationed at Hurlburt Field, Florida, and Cannon AFB, New Mexico. Two pilots, a combat systems officer (CSO) and a tactical systems officer (TSO) operate the U-28A and its systems.

U-28As at Little Rock, having evacuated to avoid a hurricane. USAF/SSgt Jeremy McGuffin

CV-22B Osprey

The CV-22B is the special operations forces' variant of the tilt-rotor Osprey and was developed in parallel with the US Marine Corps' MV-22B.

Operated by AFSOC, the Osprey can carry 18 combat-ready personnel over 538nm (996km) and return. The self-deployable tilt-rotor enables aircrews to execute long-range special operations sorties that include infiltration, exfiltration and resupply missions for SOF personnel. With a single aerial refueling it can self-deploy up to 2,100nm (3,889km) from base. It combines the vertical take-off, hover and vertical landing qualities of a helicopter with the long-range, fuel efficiency and speed characteristics of a turboprop aircraft.

The Osprey entered operational USAF service in January 2007, when the 1st Special Operations Wing at Hurlburt Field, Florida, received its first CV-22B. The tilt-rotor achieved initial operating capability with the 8th Special Operations Squadron in March 2009 and conducted its maiden operational deployment when six Ospreys arrived in Afghanistan to support Operation 'Enduring Freedom' during March 2010.

The CV-22B is powered by the same two Rolls-Royce AE1107C turboshaft engines as the MV-22B. It features the AN/APQ-186 terrain-following radar, EO/IR sensor and other advanced avionics systems that allow it to operate at low altitude in adverse weather conditions and in medium- to high-threat environments.

Numerous planned upgrades include communication, navigation, surveillance and air traffic management (CNS/ATM) modifications, enhanced navigation accuracy and upgrades for the identification friend or foe (IFF) system. The CV-22B will be equipped with the AN/APQ-187 Silent Knight radar beginning in 2021 and the system will be retrofitted to the entire fleet by 2027. The effort will be included as part of the CV-22B Block 30 upgrade. The command is considering arming the CV-22B with offensive weapons and testing to that end has already been conducted.

AFSOC's fleet of 50 CV-22Bs is shared by three operational squadrons and the formal training unit. Whereas the bulk of the aircraft are assigned to the operational units, nine Ospreys support training efforts at Kirtland AFB, New Mexico. The operational CV-22Bs are stationed at three locations in CONUS and in the United Kingdom. Citing a shortage of personnel, the plan to field a fourth squadron at Yokota Air Base, near Tokyo, Japan has been pushed out to 2020.

Squadron	Location	Aircraft	Wing/Group	Command	Tail code
7th SOS	RAF Mildenhall, Suffolk, England	CV-22B	352nd SOW/752nd SOG	AFSOC	
8th SOS	Hurlburt Field, Florida	CV-22B	27th SOW/SOG	AFSOC	
14th WPS (see note 1)	Hurlburt Field, Florida	CV-22B	57th Wing/USAFWS	ACC	
20th SOS	Cannon AFB, New Mexico	CV-22B	27th SOW/SOG	AFSOC	
71st SOS	Kirtland AFB, New Mexico	CV-22B	58th SOW/OG	AETC	
Air National Guard units					
188th RQS (see note 2)	Kirtland AFB, New Mexico	CV-22B	150th SOW/OG	AETC	

1   Utilizes aircraft assigned to host wing.
2   Associate unit conducts training alongside the active-duty 71st SOS.

A CV-22B Osprey of the 7th SOS. Jamie Hunter